Doris Stokes, the celebrated clairaudient, passed over on 8 May 1987 shortly after completing this book, her seventh volume of autobiography. Throughout her years as a medium she confounded sceptics with the uncanny accuracy of her readings and became internationally famous due to her numerous sell-out demonstrations and her many television and radio appearances both here and abroad.

In her books she has described how she first discovered her extraordinary gift and how she has shared it with the world.

Also by Doris Stokes

DORIS STOKES
with Linda Dearsley

Joyful Voices

Futura

A *Futura* Book

First published in Great Britain in 1987
by Futura Publications, a Division of
Macdonald & Co (Publishers) Ltd
London & Sydney

ISBN 0 7088 3363 2

Typeset by Leaper & Gard Ltd, Bristol
Printed in Great Britain by
Hazel, Watson & Viney Ltd
Aylesbury, Bucks

Futura Publications
A Division of
Macdonald & Co (Publishers) Ltd
Greater London House
Hampstead Road
London NW1 7QX

A BPCC plc Company

'You can't die for the life of you ...'
Doris Stokes

Chapter One

It must have been mid-afternoon when we saw him. John and I were having a sit-down after lunch and we lay back in our armchairs, staring out of the patio doors into the garden.

I was trying to tune in, in the hope of picking up a spirit contact to start me off at my demonstration that evening. I was appearing at Wembley Conference Centre. It was a big place and I was anxious in case I arrived there and nothing happened. If I could get just one little message to open the evening, I knew I would be all right.

John, who has been a healer ever since his spirit guide appeared in our bedroom and insisted that he start using his healing gift, had no such worries. He was relaxing and letting his lunch go down before tackling an afternoon's healing session. Terry was out taking Boots for a long walk.

So there we were, just the two of us, watching the birds squabbling over the crumbs on the bird-table when, suddenly, we both saw a man walk past the kitchen window towards the side door which leads into the sitting-room.

'Oh, Terry's back,' said John.

'He wasn't gone long,' I said, abandoning all hope of tuning in. I knew I wouldn't be able to concentrate with Terry and Boots jumping about all over the place. 'He said they were going to walk miles today.'

John shrugged and we waited for the side door to open, shattering our peace. But it didn't. Nothing happened.

'That's funny,' I said. 'Why haven't they come in?'

But even as I said it I realized that we'd heard no footsteps and there'd been no excited bark of greeting from Boots. In fact we hadn't even seen the man's face.

'John …' I began, but John was up and out the side door.

'There's no one here,' said John in bewilderment, staring up and down the empty patio.

'John …'

'Where can he have got to?'

'John – I think …'

But before I could stop him, John raced round to the back gate and then out into the front garden. There was no one to be seen there either. But he's nothing if not persistent, my John. The garage door was open so he searched the garage and then got down on his hands and knees on the ground to look under the car, though why he thought the man should have hidden underneath our car I can't imagine.

I was killing myself laughing by this time.

'John!' I called. 'You won't find him. You've just seen your first spirit person!'

I tuned in again and I was just able to pick up our visitor although I didn't see him again.

'I came to talk to you in the night,' said a man's voice.

'Oh, it was you, was it?' I'd woken up at ten past

three that morning with the feeling that someone was mentally tugging my sleeve.

'Doris, this is John,' a man's voice had said out of the darkness. 'Pat's very poorly, you know. Tell them that we're with Pat.'

And then he was gone, leaving me to get back to sleep as best I could.

The actress Pat Phoenix, who was a personal friend of mine, was seriously ill with lung cancer at this time and at first I took the message to be a warning that she wasn't long for this world. I'd guessed as much myself but it made me very sad to think of it. But on this occasion, I now discovered, I'd got the wrong end of the stick. I always was a one for jumping to conclusions.

'So it's John again, is it?' I asked.

'Yes,' he agreed. 'They'll all be there tonight, you know, and Pat is very poorly. You will remember to tell them about Pat. We're with her.'

So it wasn't my Pat he was talking about. It was another Pat unknown to me.

'Yes of course I'll tell them,' I assured him.

Then he mumbled something about a football team, which I didn't catch, and part of an address. It sounded like '14 Orelia Gardens'. And then he faded out again.

Well, I thought, it's not much to go on but with a bit of luck it'll get me started tonight.

I did try to tune in again but it got me nowhere. In fact, I began to think that the spirit people were having a bit of a game with me because every time I tuned in, all I could hear was a chorus of voices singing: 'Here we go, here we go, here we go …'

'Look, I know I'm going to Wembley but I do wish you'd shut up about it,' I told them crossly after the umpteenth rendering, which was not even particularly tuneful to my mind.

It was no use.. At the word 'Wembley', they launched enthusiastically into a fresh verse ... 'Here we go, here we go, here we go ...'

'Oh, I give up,' I cried. It was no use my trying to work. I might as well go and make a sandwich for tea.

If I'd been nervous before going to Wembley, I was petrified when I arrived and saw the size of the place. It was enormous.

John and I had left in plenty of time because we knew how difficult crossing London can be and consequently we arrived before Laurie (my friend and manager) and had to find our own way about. It was pretty daunting. The new building seemed to have several entrances and John and I trailed about, carrying my stage dress in its flapping polythene bag, looking for the right one.

Eventually we came to the stage-door where a kind man directed us.

'Now you want to go up those stairs,' he said, pointing to the flight behind him, 'turn right, then left and keep going.'

'Right, then left and keep going,' I reminded John as we climbed the stairs and admired the beautifully-polished brass handrail.

We followed the instructions to the letter and found ourselves in a long, silent corridor, studded with endless bright-red doors. On and on we walked, each scarlet door looking exactly like the last, until I felt thoroughly bewildered. It was like something out of *Alice in Wonderland*. Perhaps this corridor went on for ever.

Then, just as I was beginning to feel that we'd taken a wrong turning somewhere and might easily spend the whole night parading amongst eerie red doors, John stopped abruptly.

'Here we are, love. This must be it.'

Relief. At last he'd found a door that was different to the others. It said: 'Doris Stokes.'

Inside was a beautiful, modern dressing-room, complete with shower and bathroom, and there was also a comfortable Green Room for us to use. Green Rooms can sometimes be a bit scruffy, but this one was smartly decorated with what looked like green velvet on the walls. There was a bar and several small tables covered in spotless white cloths, just like a restaurant.

'Oh look, John – look at that photo on the wall,' I said, spotting a familiar face. 'That's Jack Jones.'

I'd met Jack when I was in Los Angeles. Then nearby I saw another photograph. It was Ernie Wise. I'd met Ernie too, at a Children of Courage carol service. Round the room I went, discovering more and more famous faces. I'd met this one, I knew that one, I'd always dreamed of meeting him! And so on until it was almost time for me to go on stage. I couldn't believe how quickly the minutes passed.

I didn't escape stage-fright entirely though. Interesting though the Green Room had been, there is no getting away from that terrible moment when you're standing in the wings waiting to go on and you feel so dreadfully alone.

Fortunately it soon passed. All at once the announcement was finished. My feet started walking with a will of their own and before I knew it I was standing on the stage at Wembley dressed in my finery and breathing in the sweet perfume of the flowers which, together with a comfortable chair, form my only props.

I was trembling inside, as usual, at the sight of all those people (two thousand, five hundred and twelve, they told us afterwards). But at least I had something to talk to them about, and with a bit of luck, someone out there in the audience would recognise the names, John and Pat, and the address: 14 Orelia Gardens.

'... And so you see, John saw his first spirit person today ...' I said, as I finished the story of our mysterious visitor. But even as I was speaking the words were drowned out in my head by those infuriating, singing voices.

'Here we go, here we go, here we go ...'

I was about to dismiss it impatiently when Ramanov, my spirit guide who is always there when I need him, cut in.

'No. Listen, child. Don't be hasty. This means something.'

I paused. What on earth could it mean? It sounded like nonsense to me but you never know with the spirit world. Things that don't seem to make sense at all can often prove to be amazingly significant to other people. The only thing to do was try it on the audience.

'They're at it again! Here we go, here we go, here we go ...' I said out loud, 'and I think it must mean something other than the fact that we're at Wembley. So can anybody place this contact ... a man called John, something to do with a football team and the address: 14 Orelia Gardens?'

A movement out there in that sea of faces caught my eye and, as I watched, an attractive middle-aged woman detached herself from the seats and came hurrying down to the front.

'It's for me, Doris, I think,' she said, 'only the address is Aurelia Gardens – not Orelia.'

'Well at least we found you, love.' I knew she was the right contact because the moment she reached the microphone the football chant swelled deafeningly in my ear.

'And what does, "Here we go, here we go," mean?'

The woman burst out laughing. 'They've been singing that to me at work.'

'What – today?'

'Yes. All day. Every time my trip to Wembley was mentioned they started singing it.'

'I couldn't help laughing myself. I knew exactly how she must have felt.

'And who's John?'

'John's my husband.'

The moment she used his name, I felt my spirit visitor return. I couldn't see him this time but I could sense him standing right beside me. His presence jogged my memory.

'They're very concerned about Pat, you know,' I said, 'she's very poorly indeed.'

'Yes, she is,' the woman agreed.

And satisfied that I'd kept my word, John started joining in. He gave me the name Lillian.

'That's me!' said the woman, obviously thrilled. 'I'm Lillian.'

Then the name Dave came through and the fact that he wanted to wish Dave a happy birthday.

'That's right, Dave's his friend and his birthday's

13

coming up,' Lillian confirmed.

John was really getting into his stride now. He was a wonderful communicator with a great sense of fun. He kept wandering over to give his wife a hug and then rushing back to speak to me. He started talking about the football team again and there was something about the cheeky way he said it that made me feel it was some kind of joke.

'He's mentioned this football team again,' I said, rather perplexed because I still hadn't been able to catch the whole message. 'It seems to have some special significance because he keeps going on about it.'

'Well, Dave's got a football team,' said Lillian. 'Dave's the treasurer.'

It seemed a likely explanation. I was prepared to accept it but John wasn't.

'No, no,' he said, just as frustrated as I was at my inability to get it right. 'That's not what I meant. It's a joke.'

'Well, I'm sorry, but I don't know what you mean, love.'

'It's a joke. There's eleven of them,' he said.

I passed this on and Lillian suddenly clapped her hand over her mouth and fell about laughing.

'I know what he means! There's eleven of them at work booked to come and see you at your appearance at Lewisham Theatre!'

'And that's a football team ...?' I said slowly, light dawning at last. 'John – you're a right old kidder.'

John was having a good laugh now and just to cap it, to prove we were on the right track, he gave me the name Mo.

'Yes. That's my boss at work,' explained Lillian.

14

It was quite obvious that John kept a very close eye on his family indeed. He knew everything they were doing, including the costumes they wore to fancy-dress parties.

He mentioned the name of his son Grant and of Grant's girlfriend, Tracey, and then he said something about a policeman.

'No, he means a policewoman!' said Lillian, collapsing into giggles again. 'Tracey's just been to a fancy-dress party dressed as a policewoman.'

'That's right. I know what they get up to,' said John proudly. 'Just because they can't see me, it doesn't mean I'm not around.'

He gave me some more names and family news, including the fact that his sister-in-law, Betty, had been to the hospital – again.

'Nice woman,' he said, 'but she's never happier than when she's being examined or having something done.'

By this time Lillian couldn't speak for laughing and I gathered that John had given a pretty accurate picture of his sister-in-law. But he hadn't come simply to joke and lark about. Pat wasn't far from his thoughts and it wouldn't be long, he told me, before she would be joining him.

Now how do I say that? I thought. I don't want to upset anybody if they don't know.

'Pat is very poorly, love,' I said to Lillian, stressing the 'very'.

'Yes. We know she's terminal, Doris.'

I was relieved. I could pass John's message on without fear. 'They're waiting for her and preparing her a place,' I explained. 'John would like you to take her some flowers from him and to tell her to keep her chin up because there's nothing to it. He says he suffered very badly himself before he went over and he's so glad to feel well again now.'

Lillian nodded, taking it all in, and I knew that very soon Pat would be receiving those flowers. But by now I was beginning to feel a bit guilty about the amount of time John was taking up. He was such a good communicator it was a pleasure to talk to him and he successfully kept other spirit people from elbowing him aside with their own messages. Nevertheless, it was only fair to let other members of the audience have a turn.

'Well now, John ...' I said, ready to thank him and move on.

'I know, I know,' said John, 'but just one more thing before I go.'

A deep sense of concern flooded through me and, at the same time, I found myself looking at a picture of an unusual building. At first I couldn't make out what it was. Then I saw a pigeon fly into it and I realised it was a pigeon loft.

A pigeon loft? I've been shown some strange things by spirit people in my time, but never a pigeon loft. Still, as Ramanov keeps telling me, mine is not to reason why. I stared at the little building a moment longer and, as I did so, I felt a deep ache down my right side.

'This sounds silly but you don't keep pigeons do you, love?' I asked Lillian, although she didn't look that sort of woman at all. 'Only he's showing me a pigeon loft now, and when I look at it I ache all down my right side.'

'Lillian's eyes grew round with amazement. 'I don't. It's Dave. He's building a pigeon loft. He's just started building it in his garden.'

'And does he have a job to lift his arm?'

'Yes, he does,'

So that was the reason for John's concern. Dave got angry and fed up with his problem and sometimes he was reduced to swearing in frustration.

'John says he is going to get better, you know,' I told Lillian, 'but, in the meantime, tell him when things get tough to sit down and say, "Come on John, give us a hand."'

Lillian promised to pass this on to Dave, and John, pleased to have got through so well, finally moved off the vibration to let other spirit people have a turn.

I was sorry in a way to lose him. He'd given me such a marvellous start to the evening, but I had to be fair to the others, and by now there were quite a few spirit voices clamouring in the background.

Everything went well that night. At half-time there was a hot cup of tea waiting for us in the Green Room and when I emerged on to the stage afterwards, the voices were back, clear and strong. There was a father who wanted to reassure his grown-up daughter that he'd seen her new-born baby. There was a little boy called Jason who had been tragically killed in an accident, and there was a much-loved husband who had passed with leukaemia and who wanted his wife to know that she had nothing with which to reproach herself.

Apparently she was tormented with guilt because, during her husband's illness, her fear and grief had caused her to lose her temper with him at times. She's bitterly regretted it ever since and could find no peace until she knew she was forgiven.

And so it went on. Small messages of love and affection that meant so much to their recipients.

We even had one case which indirectly answered a question I'm asked many times. People who have been married more than once often want to know which partner they'll end up with in the spirit world. Well, the lady standing nervously at the microphone sorted that one out straight away. She had been married twice, lost both husbands through illness, and now they had come back together to speak to her.

I got the names Bill and Charlie. Apparently Charlie had passed first, some years before, and then Bill had gone over just over nine weeks ago. Poor Bill had suffered very badly with cancer of the stomach but he was glad to say that he was now free of pain and full of energy once more.

He talked of his funeral – because spirit people are usually fascinated to attend their own funerals – and he knew that there had been a mix-up over the flowers and the cars.

'She got a bit upset about that,' he confided, 'but she needn't have worried. It didn't matter a bit.'

Most important of all, they wanted their wife to know that they were together.

'Charlie came to meet me, you know, when I passed,' said Bill.

Charlie agreed that this was so. 'It was grand for me to be able to thank Bill for looking after her.' he said.

It was quite clear that they both loved their wife dearly and, when her time comes, they will both be there to lead her gently into the spirit world. Jealousy seems to fade away on the other side. All that counts is love.

The evening ended in a tremendous burst of applause and cheering – so much so that the manager came over to ask when I'd come back!

'D'you think she liked it here?' he asked Laurie. 'D'you think she'd like to come back?'

I certainly would. The theatre was clean and comfortable and the audience was marvellous. Once again, I was delighted to see that so many young people had bothered to turn out for an old girl like me!

'Look at those two cockatoos!' someone said afterwards, nodding towards two young punks who were making their way towards the exit, their hair standing up in stiff spikes on top of their heads for all the world as if they'd just seen a ghost.

But what did it matter what they looked like? They'd sat there quietly and politely throughout the demonstration and they were obviously interested. We couldn't ask for anything more. How they chose to dress was their business. I don't suppose they would have wanted my hair-style any more than I would have wanted theirs!

I went back to the dressing-room as I always do, to flop, have a reviving cup of tea and a cigarette. Then, drained but happy, I collected up my things and stepped out into the night. Before I could reach the car a young lad pushed forward and thrust a potted plant into my arms.

He was only seventeen and he'd been waiting an hour and a half outside the stage-door to give it to me.

I was touched. How can you criticize young people when they do such lovely things? I thanked the boy, and clutching the plant and my dress I climbed awkwardly into the car.

Well, after all my nerves, Wembley had certainly

made me feel welcome. And as we pulled away past the famous stadium, I found myself humming a familiar tune, 'Here we go, here we go, here we go ...'

Chapter Two

It was the laugh that did it. I'd gone into the bathroom to clean the sink and I was just taking off my
new, 'good' wedding-ring, the way I always do so it
doesn't get spoiled by scouring powder, when suddenly this rich, warm laughter spilled out behind me.

I almost dropped the ring in surprise. Automatically, I turned round but of course there was no-one
there. The room was quite empty. In fact the whole
house was empty except for me. John had taken Boots
out for his morning walk and Terry was at work.
Could Jean have popped in unheard, I wondered
briefly, but then I dismissed the thought. No, she
would have knocked first.

Besides, that wasn't Jean's laugh. There was only
one person I knew who laughed like that and that was
Pat Phoenix – kind, warm-hearted Pat Phoenix who
had passed over the day before.

Quickly I put my ring on the top of the cistern for
safety and this action brought a fresh chuckle from my
unseen visitor.

'That's right, love,' said a friendly voice. 'you look
after it.'

'Is that you, Pat?' I asked, rather unnecessarily
because there was no mistaking that vibrant tone. 'Are
you okay?'

'Yes, I'm okay, kid,' she said, 'I just wanted you to tell Tony to keep the ring, the one I married him with. I was very fond of that ring. I don't mind about the other things but I would like him to keep that. Tell him to put it on a chain.'

'Don't worry, Pat, I'll tell him,' I assured her.

And then all at once, that indefinable feeling of electricity went out of the air and I knew I was alone in the bathroom again.

'Pat?' I said experimentally just in case I'd made a mistake. But there was no answer. She'd gone.

It was so unexpected and so brief, I felt quite frustrated. If only I'd had a bit more warning I'd have been prepared for a longer chat. Still, that's the spirit world for you. You can't force spirit people to work to appointments. They pop in and out when they've got the time. And it was very good that Pat was able to get a message through so soon after her passing. It takes quite a bit of effort.

I abandoned the sink and went off to phone the Booth's home with the news. Pat's husband, Tony Booth, was in deep mourning of course. I didn't want to disturb him, so instead I passed the message on to Kitty, Pat's loyal friend and housekeeper.

'Just tell Tony we're thinking of him and that I hope the message will be of some comfort,' I said when I'd explained.

And Kitty, who was naturally very distressed herself because she'd loved Pat too, promised that she would.

It was a sad time. We'd been expecting the worst for some time, of course, but nevertheless it's always a blow when it comes.

Over the last few weeks I'd got into the habit of phoning the hospital now and then to see how Pat

22

was, and just the day before she passed, about five o'clock in the afternoon, I had a sudden impulse to ring the ward. When someone is as ill as poor Pat was it's wise not to ignore such impulses. I had a dreadful feeling that she'd taken a turn for the worse.

'Hello, nurse, it's Doris Stokes here,' I said when I was put through to the ward. 'I don't want to be put through to Pat's room, I'm just ringing to ask if you could give Pat and Tony my love.'

'Of course I will, Mrs Stokes,' said the nurse.

'And how is Pat today?'

There was a tiny pause and then came the professional nurse's trained response. 'There's no change,' she said, matter-of-factly.

But I wasn't going to be fobbed off like that. After all I'd been a nurse myself. 'She's not very well, is she, love?' I persisted.

There was another slight hesitation and then I got through to the real person underneath the professional exterior.

'Well, no, I'm afraid she's not, Mrs Stokes,' the nurse admitted.

'Oh dear. I thought as much,' I said. 'Well could you tell her that we're thinking of her and praying for her?'

'I'd be glad to, Mrs Stokes,' said the nurse.

The next morning chaos broke out in the Stokes household. It so happened that we'd arranged to have our carpets cleaned that day. They hadn't been down very long but they'd had to stand up to a growing puppy rushing around with muddy paws and having the odd 'accident', and they were looking distinctly grimy.

Anyway, just after breakfast three men and a van

23

arrived with a great big hose affair. Boots, of course, had never seen anything like it and he started to charge about, barking his head off. John went to see if there was anything he could do, got tangled up with everyone and added to the confusion. Terry decided he'd better make a big pot of tea and then Jean arrived to help with the cleaning.

It seemed as if there were people and dogs everywhere. I bustled about trying to clear furniture out of the way without tripping over anyone and then, in the midst of it all, the phone rang.

'Hello, Doris,' said a voice, 'this is the ...'

'I'm sorry,' I shouted, putting one hand over my free ear. 'Can you speak up a bit? I can't hear you, it's a bit noisy here.'

'... the *Manchester Evening News*,' repeated the man. 'We just wondered if you'd heard ... Pat Phoenix passed away at 8.45 this morning.'

I sat down heavily in an armchair that had been pushed against the wall.

'No. No, I hadn't heard,' I said. 'I'm very sorry.'

I had been expecting it, of course, but I was shocked just the same. I felt a bit guilty too. It was terrible to think that Pat had slipped away while my back was turned, as it were, at a time when I was so preoccupied with the upheaval at home that I hadn't even given her a thought. I didn't even send up a prayer for her this morning, I realized in shame. Pat would forgive me, I knew that, but I still felt bad.

It got worse as the day went on. By mid-morning the phone was red hot and it didn't stop ringing until late in the evening. Newspaper after newspaper, knowing of my friendship with Pat, rang to ask for a 'tribute' to her. A few minutes' conversation, how-

24

ever, soon established that they didn't really want a tribute, they wanted to know if Pat had come back to talk to me.

The reporters turned the questions around and wheedled away, trying to get me to say that I'd had contact with Pat. But I couldn't say that because it wasn't true. I hadn't heard a word from Pat and I didn't expect to.

It's very difficult to get people to understand that I can't just ring the spirit world and have a chat to anybody I choose. When the time is right spirit people will make contact with their loved ones – except in a few unusual cases, love is the link that makes it work. Now Pat and I were very fond of each other but uppermost in her mind as she started her new life in the spirit world would be people like Tony, her husband, not me.

'I'm sorry, love,' I explained for the umpteenth time to a reporter, 'it doesn't work like that. I haven't heard from Pat and I don't suppose I will.'

Which just goes to show, as I've often said, how wrong a medium can be. Pat came to speak to me the very next day but only because she wanted to get a message through to Tony and she knew that I would be able to pass it on easily because I had their home telephone number.

I first met Pat some years ago when I was invited to appear on the Russell Harty Show. As I explained in one of my earlier books, the show proceeded quite normally until, towards the end, Russell sprang a little surprise on me.

'Now,' he said, with a merry glint in his eye, 'we have a surprise mystery guest here tonight. We thought it would be a bit of fun if Doris could discover her identity.'

I was rather taken aback, I must admit, because identifying mystery guests is not something I do. I had no idea if it would work or not. In fact I had a nasty suspicion that it wouldn't, but I've never been able to resist a challenge so I said I'd have a go.

The mystery guest was hidden away somewhere at the back of the studio and I was linked to her by telephone.

'Hello, Doris,' said an Irish voice, sweet as honey.

'Hello, love,' I replied calmly, but inside I was quaking. This was going to be impossible. I didn't have a clue. I'd been to Ireland a few times but I hadn't met this lady, I was sure. I didn't recognize her voice at all. What's more the clock was ticking away and I knew we only had a moment or two before the show ended.

'Be careful,' said Ramanov, my guide, breaking into my panic, 'the accent's not genuine.'

It had me fooled. Nevertheless, if Ramanov said it was a phoney accent then phoney it must be.

'I don't think that's your real voice,' I said slowly to the mystery lady.

'Oh, sure it is,' she insisted.

'No, I have a feeling you don't normally speak like that,' I said. 'In fact I think you're an actress.'

Every time she spoke, her spirit people came closer and I was suddenly aware of a lady in a wheelchair.

'Yes, I know who that is,' said the Irish voice when I told her.

'And I'm getting the name Minnie or Mimi.'

Again the mystery guest agreed that she knew who I meant.

'Pat,' whispered a voice close by.

26

'Who's Pat?' I asked, thinking it was someone the guest knew.

There was a tiny hesitation.

'Yes, I know a Pat,' the guest admitted.

Then I stopped. There was something wrong here. Surely Pat was the name of the guest herself, not a friend or relative. Time was running out. Should I risk a guess? Could it be Patti Coombs?

'Sorry,' said Russell Harty, stepping in quickly and cutting me off. 'That's all we've got time for, I'm afraid. And now here is our mystery guest.'

I craned forward eagerly, and out from behind the screen came, not Patti Coombs but Pat Phoenix.

Disappointment at having failed to identify the guest in the time available melted away. I was thrilled. *Coronation Street* was one of my favourite programmes and, at that time, Pat, who was in it every week playing Elsie Tanner, was the character I loved best.

'Never mind, Doris,' said Pat, 'if you'd had more time you would have got me. You were getting so close!'

We had a long chat after the show and we became friends from that moment.

Pat was a wonderful lady. She could be fiery-tempered and could blow up in a moment if something annoyed her but the next minute she was sorry and looking for a way to make amends. She always had time for the underdog and she was one of the most generous people I've ever known.

'God, it's only money,' she used to say as she bought yet another expensive present for someone.

She always had time to listen, too, and if she sensed you were feeling a bit depressed she did her best to

27

buck you up.

'I get so embarrassed about my shaky leg,' I confided one night when she rang shortly before I was due to leave for a theatre appearance. For some reason, ever since my stroke, my leg has had a tendency to shake uncontrollably and to my chagrin it often decides to do it when I'm sitting on the stage talking to an audience.

'Forget about that, love,' said Pat 'You just go out there and slay 'em. You've got your work to do. Once you get going they'll be listening to you – not looking at your leg.'

She was always very kind. Soon after we met on the Russell Harty Show she sent me a beautiful, signed photograph of herself and I put it proudly on my bookcase. You couldn't miss it when you walked into my sitting-room. Well, naturally, visitors noticed it and invariably they said: 'Oh do you know Pat Phoenix? I love her.'

And some were such great fans they begged for the chance just to say hello to her. It was very hard to resist and occasionally when I knew she wasn't too busy, I'd phone Pat and ask if she would help.

'Pat, I've got so-and-so here,' I'd explain, 'd'you think you could just say hello, it would mean so much to her.'

And Pat, bless her, never refused. 'Of course I will, Doris,' she would say and would patiently chat to whoever it was I put on the line.

She was generous in every way: with her money, her time and her genuine delight in the good fortune of others. When she heard I'd been able to buy my own house at last after a lifetime in rented accommodation, she was almost as thrilled as I was.

'Not before time, Doris,' she said. 'You enjoy it, love. You deserve it. I know what you do for people and what you give.'

Pat hadn't had an easy life, perhaps that's why she was able to be so compassionate to others, but at last things were going well for her. She had sorted out her career and was tackling all kinds of new and exciting roles. And at last, after years of being unlucky in love, she'd found happiness with Tony Booth. They had their fights, of course, but then doesn't any couple in love? Making up was all the sweeter.

Yes, things had come right for Pat. It seemed so unfair that at this time when she ought to have been enjoying herself, she should be struck down by lung cancer. I was very, very sad when I heard the news, particularly when the hospital announced that they wouldn't be giving her any treatment. That meant they didn't hold out much hope.

Yet despite the gravity of the situation, Pat still found time to think of others. I phoned her in hospital to try to cheer her up a bit and all she could think of was her friend Pauline, who'd popped in to see her.

'Doris, do me a favour, will you?' she asked.

'Of course I will if I can, Pat,' I assured her.

'Well I've got this friend here who's just arrived, her name's Pauline and I wondered if you'd have a word with her. She came to see you in Manchester – I was coming with her but then I had to go to London to rehearse – anyway, she thought you were marvellous and she'd love to say hello.'

What a small request, I thought, and how could I possibly refuse after the many times Pat had done the same for me.

'I'll talk to her with pleasure, Pat,' I said warmly.

I spoke to Pauline for a few minutes and then Pat came back on the line.

'Oh thank you, Doris,' she said. 'That's made her day.'

And I thought to myself, 'What a wonderful girl you are, Pat. In spite of all you've got to put up with you still think of your friends.'

Pat didn't ask for anything for herself, but the spirit world would let me know if there was any tiny way in which I could cheer her up. The first time I sent flowers to the hospital, I ordered them by phone, and half-way through my instructions to the florist, I stopped.

I'd been planning a gorgeous display of pink and white flowers but all I could think of was teddy bears.

'D'you think you could go out and buy a teddy bear and put it in the basket of flowers?' I asked slowly. I couldn't think what made me say it but suddenly it seemed very important that Pat should have a teddy bear.

The florist promised to do as I asked and I could only hope that Pat would be pleased.

Pat *was* pleased. I discovered afterwards that, that very afternoon, Pat had looked around her room which was overflowing with flowers because so many people loved her and said, 'There are so many flowers. I wish someone would send me a teddy bear.'

And ten minutes later my flowers arrived, complete with a pink teddy bear sitting in the basket. I didn't know it then, but apparently Pat used to collect teddy bears and one day she lent her collection to a charity and they got lost. She never saw them again.

Tony told me about this afterwards when he rang to thank me for the flowers, to save Pat tiring herself

30

with too many phone calls. Through Tony I discovered that the bear Pat missed most was her beloved Paddington.

That did it. I was determined that Pat's Paddington should be replaced at all costs. I knew there wasn't much time left so Laurie, Terry and I started scouring London. There had been a run on Paddingtons, it seemed, and for a while it looked as if we were out of luck. Shop after shop declared themselves sold out. Then we found a place that had two Paddingtons left and Laurie raced over to claim one of them.

I had this terrible feeling that Pat wouldn't have long to enjoy her new bear and I wanted her to have it as soon as she possibly could, so Terry very kindly offered to fly up to Manchester and deliver it personally to the hospital.

I know Pat was pleased. I was very touched a few days later to see a photograph taken at Pat's last press conference in which she was holding a few teddy bears and there amongst them was Paddington.

I only spoke to her once more before she passed over and by then her illness was really taking its toll.

'Oh, Doris, what a thing,' she said wearily, 'I've been on oxygen today.'

'Never mind, darling,' I said, 'as long as it helps you breathe.'

I didn't keep her. I didn't want her to use up her strength talking to me.

That night I couldn't sleep for thinking about Pat. I was sure she was having a bad night and as I tossed and turned, a little poem about Paddington Bear came into my head.

It was only a silly little rhyme but I thought it might make her smile and so I got up and wrote it down.

The next day I phoned Tony and read it to him.

'I haven't brought you flowers tied up with golden string,

'I haven't brought you perfume or a diamond ring,

'But here I come with my wellies on with a heart as big as a bucket,

'Filled to the brim with love for you and a message – 'Dear Pat, sock it!'

Tony roared with laughter when I'd finished. 'She'll love that, Doris,' he said.

And I can only hope that it brightened her day a little.

Pat's last wish came true, I'm glad to say, when she married Tony Booth in a moving and beautiful little ceremony at her bedside. She passed over peacefully soon afterwards as Mrs Booth.

It annoyed me rather when I read later that her priest had said, 'She turned to God in the end,' as if Pat had belatedly discovered religion. In fact, Pat had never turned away from God. She believed implicitly in life after death and she'd had several personal experiences of the spirit world.

Soon after I met her for the first time she gave a long interview to *Psychic News* in which she described how she saw a ghost in her own home.

Apparently, Pat had bought an old Georgian house in Sale, near Manchester, and she was busy restoring it to its former splendour.

One night she was sitting watching television when

suddenly she heard a muffled thud from upstairs. She wasn't alarmed. Old houses are never silent and she thought something had probably fallen over in the bedroom.

Then about twenty minutes later she glanced up from the television screen and saw an old lady walk past the open door. For a moment she thought it must be her cleaner – then she realized it was far too late for any cleaner to be working. Something strange was obviously going on. Surely it couldn't be an elderly burglar?

Pat raced upstairs and searched every room. There was no one there. She ran down and searched the downstairs rooms. There was no one there either. Pat was alone in the house. She could only conclude that she'd seen a ghost.

The next evening at the same time, the same thing happened, only this time Pat noticed that her visitor seemed to be holding something in her arms.

From then on the old lady made regular appearances and Pat's mother, who often came to stay, grew so used to her that she regarded her as a friend.

Eventually, through a neighbour, they discovered the ghost's identity. Years before, an actress named Madame Muller had lived in the house. Her theatre days must have been behind her because she was reduced to giving drama and elocution lessons. She was a lonely woman. Her marriage had failed, and on warm afternoons she used to stand at the front-garden gate with her little dog in her arms, watching the world go by.

I believe that poor old Madame Muller felt a great empathy with Pat, an actress and dog-lover like herself and, what's more, a woman with a great feeling for the past who was trying to restore the house to the way it used to be. I expect she liked to drop in to see what Pat was up to and had they lived on earth at the same time, they might well have been friends.

Pat, of course, was very psychic, which is why spirit people were drawn to her and why she was able to see them.

We'll all miss Pat. She was a gutsy lady right to the end. Not for her any dreary, mournful hymns at her funeral. She arranged for a rousing rendering of 'When the Saints Come Marching In'.

I switched on the television to watch the ceremony and I was instantly reminded of a conversation we'd had months ago, long before she became ill.

Pat had phoned to ask if John and I would send out prayers to a friend of hers who needed spiritual help. I took down the details and then the conversation moved on to other things.

'Did you see that bit in the paper about the old-age pensioner who saved up for her funeral?' I asked Pat.

'No,' said Pat, 'what about her?'

'Well, I thought it was fantastic. She saved enough to hire a brass band and as the coffin was carried out of the house the band played, 'Wish Me Luck as You Wave Me Goodbye'. What a way to go. That old lady certainly did it in style. She must have been a marvellous character.'

Pat agreed that if you had to go, that was certainly the way to do it, and I think the conversation planted the idea in her mind. She too had a wonderful send-off.

At around this time I opened *The Sun* newspaper and came face to face with a marvellous cartoon. Chatting and sipping their drinks in a cosy pub were

Ena Sharples, Albert Tatlock, Jack Walker and other members of the *Coronation Street* cast who've passed over. On the window was the name, The Spirits Return, and walking in through the open door was Pat Phoenix.

'I thought I'd find you lot in here,' Pat is saying.

And I had to smile. Pat would enjoy that no end, I thought. I bet she's laughing her head off up there.

Chapter Three

It was a terrible moment. A few words, carelessly spoken on the telephone, suddenly pitched me into a nightmare.

'You know this case where the little girl's disappeared, Doris,' Laurie said casually, after bringing me up to date with my work for the coming week. 'Any idea what's happened to her?'

I hadn't. I'd heard the story on the news, of course. Six-year-old Collette Gallacher had left the house on Friday morning to catch the school bus at the stop just a few minutes from her home and she hadn't been seen since. She hadn't set foot on the bus and she didn't reach school that day.

I sympathized with the parents and, like most of us in these dreadful times, I feared the worst for the poor child because such awful things go on these days. But I didn't know. I'd had no eerie forebodings. I knew no more about the case than anyone else.

And then Laurie came out with that casual question.

'No, Laurie,' I started to say, 'I hope she's … Oh no!' The words choked in my throat and I let out a strangled cry of horror.

As we talked I'd been looking at a vase of flowers, placed on the shelf only a few minutes before. Suddenly, as I started to talk of Collette, the beautiful pink carnation I'd been admiring turned into the face of a child. The face of a very dead child.

She had dark, almost black hair and huge dark eyes from which the life had already departed. I was looking at a body. The child, little Collette Gallacher, had made her journey into the spirit world.

Then there was a sort of jerk, the child's face disappeared, and I was looking at a street, a plain, small town street that could have been anywhere.

'She's only four doors away,' a voice said loudly.

Abruptly the street faded and I had the sensation of bumping up a lot of stairs, climbing high.

'She's in the top room,' the voice added, and at the same time I felt something over my face and I couldn't breathe, I was suffocating ...

'Doris ... are you still there? Hello? Hello?'

Mercifully, I could breathe again, the awful pictures melted and I was looking at nothing more alarming than a vase of carnations.

'Oh Laurie,' I gasped.

'Doris, are you all right?' he asked anxiously.

'Yes, yes I'm fine,' I said, collecting my wits. 'But the child. It's about the child. She's over, Laurie. I'm absolutely certain of it and she's not far away.'

I told him what I'd seen. 'And the poor child's got a sock or a gag or something in her mouth,' I added, 'because I felt something over my face and I couldn't breathe.'

There was a shocked silence.

'I don't know what to say,' said Laurie after a moment or two. 'You see, the reason I asked is that I've had Collette's aunt on the phone asking if you could help find her. They're obviously still hoping that she's alive somewhere. We can't tell them what you've just said.'

'No, of course not,' I agreed. I was quite certain I was right, but supposing I wasn't? Supposing there'd been some appalling mix-up? I couldn't possibly put the parents through that torture.

Once upon a time I might have gone straight to the police but, sadly, I've learned the hard way that this is not a good idea. These days, unless the police come to me and ask me to help, I know it's better not to interfere with their investigations.

'You'll just have to be very tactful, Laurie,' I said. 'Tell them that we are praying for them and will do everything we can and should there be any bad news and they want to see me, I'll willingly see them at any time.'

I hoped the tiny hint about bad news might go some way towards preparing them for the shock to come.

Laurie agreed to be as tactful as he knew how and he was, but shortly afterwards the aunt phoned him again.

'She's been found,' she said.

Laurie sighed, 'Just a minute then, love. I can tell you now what Doris said.' And he explained to the aunt what I'd seen and why I felt it would be too distressing to pass on to the parents until the body was found.

'Well, Doris was exactly right,' said the aunt, 'except for one thing. She didn't have a sock or a gag in her mouth. It was a plastic bag over her head.'

In fact, as we found out later, it wasn't even a plastic bag. The wicked man had wrapped cling-film round the child's head. No wonder I'd felt as if I couldn't breathe.

Poor Mrs Gallacher was devastated as any mother would be, but when the first terrible grief and shock had eased slightly, she came to see me.

She arrived at the house, a tiny little woman with huge, haunted eyes. She looked like a child herself, hardly old enough to be a mother, and she'd brought with her her friend Teresa because, like many people, she didn't know what to expect.

John and I got them settled with a cup of tea and as soon as I tuned in, the chilling, goose-bumps-all-over feeling that I always get when a murder victim moves close swept over me. I shivered involuntarily. Then, to my relief, the sensation passed and a sunny, happy little soul arrived singing Happy Birthday in a sweet, childish voice.

'She's singing Happy Birthday,' I said. 'Is there a birthday in the family?'

'It's her nan's birthday today,' said Karen Gallacher.

A warm feeling of love filled the room and Collette gave me the name Anne.

'That's my mum,' said Karen.

As she talked I glanced over at Karen and briefly I saw a pretty dark head close to hers and two dark eyes beaming up at her. Whatever the poor child had gone through she was now bright as a button and chattering excitedly.

'What your mummy really wants to know is if you're all right now, darling,' I explained to her after she'd mentioned a few family members and friends. 'Are you happy?'

'I wasn't happy when I first came but now I'm all right,' said Collette.

She spent a lot of time drawing and painting, she

39

told me, and had got ever so good at it. She also liked helping with the babies and she'd achieved a long-held ambition.

'I always wanted to go and see the Queen with her crown on,' said Collette. 'Well now I just go and see her whenever I like, but she doesn't wear her crown, you know.' She sounded rather disappointed.

'No, well I think she only wears it on special occasions, love.'

'Oh, and tell Mum I've got Mrs Mac here,' Collette added, as an older person joined her and no doubt jogged her memory.

'That's my nan,' said Karen. 'She was Mrs McAlpine but everyone called her Mrs Mac.'

The child's main concern was to cheer her mother up and she avoided the subject of the murder, but after a while she couldn't help blurting out the thing that was worrying her most.

'Is Mummy angry?' she whispered.' She always told me not to go anywhere with strangers. Well, I didn't really. I went on an errand for him. But is Mummy very angry because I went into the house?'

'No one's angry with you, love,' I told her. 'No one blames you.'

'He said he wanted to give me something for going. I wouldn't have gone in otherwise.'

'No, of course you wouldn't love,' I told her. 'But let's not talk about that. What else can you tell me?'

'Mummy's moved since then,' she offered.

'Yes, I have,' said Karen.

Then she said something about hospital.

'I'm going into hospital soon,' Karen explained.

'Well, don't worry, Mum, cos I'll be there,' said Collette. 'I always used to cheer Mummy up when she was crying, you know.'

'She certainly did,' Karen agreed.

But now the subject of the murder had been mentioned, Collette wanted to talk about it. Once again I felt that dreadful suffocating feeling and she told me various things that had happened which I felt I couldn't pass on to her mother.

'No, darling, I can't tell your mummy that,' I explained, 'it will only upset her and it doesn't matter now, does it? You're all right now.'

'But why did he have to kill me?' asked Collette in genuine bewilderment.

'He was a wicked man, darling,' I explained. 'Don't dwell on it. Tell me what else is going on now.'

'There's going to be a baby,' she said more cheerfully.

'My brother's wife is having a baby,' said Karen.

So I knew that Collette would be taking a great interest in her little cousin when he or she was born.

There were more family details and then eventually Collette ended on a happy note.

'Mummy's going to meet someone,' she confided. 'In fact she's already met him and she's going to start a new life. There's going to be a wedding.'

'Well I don't know about that,' said Karen.

'If Collette says so, it must be true,' I told her. 'You write and let me know. In fact you can send me a piece of wedding-cake!'

I was glad to see the laughter come back into her careworn face.

'I'll do that, Doris,' Karen promised, 'I won't forget.'

A few weeks afterwards I heard that the sitting had made a dramatic difference to her life. Apparently all her friends commented on how much better she looked, as if a great weight had been lifted from her shoulders, and she was able to piece together the tragic story of Collette's last day.

On 26 February 1986 Collete had left home as usual in plenty of time to catch the school bus. She was six years old, a pretty child with shoulder-length hair and gaps in her teeth where her baby teeth had fallen out and her second teeth had yet to grow.

Not far from the bus-stop a neighbour, whom Collette probably knew by sight, put his head out of the front door to ask if she would buy a packet of crisps for him from the corner shop. Collette was the sort of child who would do anything for anybody and the shop was only yards away so she probably thought she had time to buy the crisps and still get back for her bus.

All the police know is that when she returned to the man's house, he took her inside, assaulted and murdered her. They found her body four days later and only then because the man, overcome with remorse, had tried to slash his wrists and left a suicide note.

The suicide attempt failed and he was sentenced to life imprisonment with a recommendation that he serve no less than twenty-five years.

'And I hope he never comes out,' said Karen Gallacher.

And who can blame her?

It took me quite a while to recover from that sitting. It's very important to help parents in cases like these but I must admit that I hate doing them. It tears my insides out. After Karen had gone I sat there looking at the photograph she'd left me of her daughter. Collette was such a beautiful child with her big, wide

42

smile and her two front teeth missing, and I thought, you poor little darling. How frightened you must have been ... What makes men do these terrible things? What's the matter with them?

I do get rather depressed with it all at times, I'm afraid, and to make matters worse, not long after I met Karen I did a demonstration at Canterbury where I came across another particularly sad case.

There was nothing wrong with Canterbury, of course. Although we didn't have time to look around you could see from the car that it was a lovely place. We passed higgledy-piggledy old timbered houses that leant drunkenly out over narrow little streets. There were picturesque shops selling all kinds of fascinating things and tiny lanes that wound tantalizingly away allowing snatched glimpses of yet more beautiful buildings. And the cathedral, of course, is legendary.

Surprisingly enough in such an old place, the theatre was quite new. Backstage it even had an unfinished air about it. I nearly had a fit when I was shown into the 'star' dressing-room. It was a long, narrow room complete with washing machine, spin-dryer and mops and buckets for decoration. It quite reminded me of the old days going round to church halls.

The main body of the theatre was beautiful, however, and the people were warm and friendly. We had a very good night but one case in particular stood out in my mind.

A young girl called Tracey came to talk to me. She even gave me part of her address: Bramley Cottage. Apparently, she'd left home to live with her boyfriend who turned out to be a bit of a swine.

'It didn't work out, Doris,' she said, 'but I was too

stubborn and too proud to go back home.'

There was something peculiar about her passing and a verdict of misadventure had been reached at the inquest. I thought it best not to delve too deeply into that at a public meeting so I asked Tracey to tell me what her parents were doing now.

'They feel guilty,' Tracey said at once. 'They keep feeling guilty and they shouldn't. Tell Mum not to feel guilty because of what they can do now.'

I found this rather puzzling but I passed it on to the mother just as I'd heard it.

'Does this mean anything to you, love?' I asked. 'Because she seems to be quite worried about it.'

The little woman at the microphone nodded her head vigorously. 'I know exactly what she means,' she said. 'When Tracey was a little girl we didn't have very much. Life was always a struggle. But now my husband has his own business and we could give Tracey everything she wanted. We have plenty of money, but what good is money to us now when we don't have a daughter?'

Her poignant words seemed to tug at my heart and they haunted me for weeks afterwards. I gave her the big floral centrepiece from the stage; a magnificent arrangement of pink and white carnations, gladioli and white chrysanthemums, as a tribute from her daughter, but I couldn't get her out of my mind.

Then a few days later a strange thing happened. I went to bed feeling depressed, thinking about Collette and Tracey and wondering for the umpteenth time why these things have to happen. As I undressed I noticed with mild surprise that the fancy pillows that I move from the bed to the armchair at night, had been taken from the chair where I left them and

44

placed on the blanket box.

Now what are they doing there? I wondered. But I was too tired to care much and certainly too tired to move them back again. Well, you can stay there till the morning, I told them wearily as I climbed between the sheets.

I stretched out my hand, turned off the lamp and I was just settling down to sleep when a shape made me gasp. There was someone sitting in the armchair.

My eyes flew open properly and by the light from the street lamps outside I saw that it was my father. He was sitting in the chair with his hands on his knees and he was smiling at me.

Strangely enough I could even see his reflection in the mirror doors of my wardrobe.

'Dad!' I cried. 'What are you doing here?'

He didn't answer, he just nodded reassuringly, as if to say, 'Everything's all right, Dol. I'm here. Go to sleep now.'

Suddenly I remembered that in addition to my depression, it was the anniversary of my long-ago, stillborn little girl. No wonder I felt down.

Yet as I looked at Dad's kind smile, the grey cloud seemed to melt away, my eyes felt unbearably heavy and I drifted off into sleep.

That night I had the best night's sleep I'd had for months and when I woke the next morning the bed looked as if it hadn't been slept in. I'd lain so still I'd hardly rumpled the sheets.

And when I looked down at the bottom of the bed I saw that the pillows had moved back from the top of the blanket box and were in their normal place in the armchair.

I felt cheerful and full of energy for the first time in

45

weeks.

'Thank you, Dad,' I said out loud, 'I needed that.'
And I went off with a light step to start the chores.

Chapter Four

It was one of the prettiest displays I'd ever seen: a miniature crib trimmed with pink and white frills and crammed to overflowing with pastel-coloured flowers and little ornamental storks.

It was absolutely beautiful but there was surely some mistake.

'But this is for someone who's just had a baby,' I protested as the receptionist tried to hand it to me.

'Well, it definitely says Doris Stokes,' she insisted.

I laughed. 'Impossibilities I'll have a try at, love,' I said, 'but miracles I leave to God!'

Nevertheless, I took the little card that was pinned to the flowers and peered at it. Sure enough it was addressed to Doris Stokes and it came with love from my new friends, Erdal and Filiz Danyal and most particularly, from their new-born daughter, Ayse.

It was such a shame. I'd been looking forward to seeing the baby and the visit was all arranged, when I managed to land myself in hospital again.

It was nothing serious, I'm glad to say. I caught a nasty flu bug while travelling round the country in November and somehow I couldn't seem to shake it off. By December I had pleurisy and, despite the fact that the doctor had given me enough pills to stock a small pharmacist's, I seemed to get worse instead of better. Then one morning I was standing in the kitchen, stirring the porridge, when suddenly I collapsed.

I gave Terry a terrible fright I must say. I'm not the fainting type so he's not exactly used to me keeling over all over the place but I'm glad he was there even though it was a nasty shock for him. It was most peculiar. One minute I was concentrating on bubbling porridge, the next the room was fading away and I was falling backwards.

'Terry help me, I'm going!' I cried, meaning that I thought I was going to faint.

Terry, unfortunately, thought I meant that I was passing over and it shook him rigid. Somehow he half carried me into the sitting-room, propped me up in a chair and then frantically phoned the doctor.

I've mentioned our marvellous doctor before in previous books. Well, he was good as ever. He only lives round the corner and he arrived at the house within ten minutes of Terry's call. By this time, of course, I was groggy but conscious, and more worried about the burnt porridge than anything else. I don't like the boys starting the day without a hot meal in their stomachs.

'Never mind the porridge,' said Dr David sternly. 'What's all this? I think this bad chest of yours has gone on long enough. We'd better get you into hospital and find out what's wrong.'

It was only a couple of weeks before Christmas and there was stacks to be done. The letters were piling up, I had a public demonstration arranged, not a single Christmas card had gone out and I hadn't even started the Christmas shopping. I couldn't have picked a more inconvenient time.

'I can't go into hospital. I'm much too busy,' I explained.

'Oh yes, you can and you must,' said Dr David.

He was backed up by John and Terry and of course I was outnumbered. While I lay back weakly drinking tea, the doctor phoned around to organize a bed, John and Terry packed a few things into a case and before I'd fully recovered my senses I was on my way to the local hospital.

I didn't realize it at the time but the doctor feared there might be something seriously wrong with my heart or my lungs. He couldn't understand why I should have passed out so unexpectedly and why my illness was not responding to treatment.

The hospital doctors were puzzled too. They gave me oxygen to help me breathe and then conducted test after test. Thankfully my heart and lungs showed no signs of serious damage. In the end they came to the conclusion that I'd fainted because my chest was so congested that when I bent over the cooker to stir the porridge, the oxygen supply to my brain was momentarily cut off. As for my illness, it was hanging around because I was exhausted.

'Oh, that's all right then,' I said in relief when they told me, 'I can go home.' And I started collecting up the things on my bedside table and searching about for my case.

'Oh no you don't,' they said. 'You're to stay here.'

They couldn't hold me against my will of course, a hospital is not a prison, but they made it quite clear that I would be mad to leave just then. If I carried on the way I'd been going I would end up with double pneumonia.

Put that way there didn't seem to be a lot of choice. There was nothing to be done but resign myself to another stay in hospital. It was such a shame Laurie had to ring round cancelling all my appointments. The letters piled up unread and the Christmas shopping had to be left to John and Terry. Goodness knows what we'll end up having for Christmas dinner with those two in charge, I thought. Still, it'll be a surprise!

Most disappointing of all was the fact that I wouldn't now be able to visit little Ayse in hospital and hold her in my arms when she was just a few hours old. I telephoned Erdal Danyal to apologize and he was most understanding.

'Never mind, Doris,' he said. 'As soon as you are better you must come and see us at home instead.'

And the next day the beautiful crib of flowers arrived to cheer me up. Actually I think the fact that I got a crib and storks was a bit of a misunderstanding on the part of the florist. I believe Erdal ordered flowers to be sent to me 'from the baby' and somewhere along the line the message got changed to 'for the baby'. But it didn't matter at all. The crib was exquisite, it gave us much more fun than a conventional bunch of flowers would have done and I shall keep it to remind me of the day Ayse was born.

I met the Danyals, as I do so many of my new friends, through a sitting. These days, I'm sorry to say, I can do very few private sittings and Erdal Danyal had been waiting a long time to see me.

Laurie arranges all the bookings from his office so I never know who's coming to see me until they arrive, but it turned out that Erdal Danyal was from Turkey and he had been given three of my books following the death of his father. He had been waiting for a sitting ever since.

I always enjoy working with overseas people because it's such a challenge. I don't speak a word of any language other than English, I'm afraid, so Ramanov (my guide) always translates the messages for me. Names, however, come in their original form as a means of identification for the sitter and it's quite a job, I can tell you, getting my tongue round some of them.

It was Erdal's mother I remember chiefly from the sitting. She had passed a few years before his father, and although I don't often see spirit people (these days I tend only to see spirit children) she communicated so strongly that I was able to catch a brief glimpse of her face. She was very much like her son with straight black hair worn in a plain style, and lively dark eyes.

Mrs Danyal senior had quite a lot to say for herself I recall, and in particular she was irritated because one of her other sons had not been able to name his boat after her.

She put into my mind a picture of a beautiful, blue sea and an island sparkling in the sun. Then she showed me a boat bobbing about on the water.

'That is my son's boat,' she said indignantly, 'and my son wanted to name it after me but his wife wouldn't let him.'

Erdal, somewhat surprised, I think, confirmed that this was true. Apparently, the family spent their holidays on this island and Erdal's brother had had a boat specially built. He had intended to name it in memory of his mother but at the last minute his wife had prevented him from doing so.

Mrs Danyal and some other members of the family chatted away for nearly two hours but since I can't remember all the details myself, I'll let Erdal explain what happened:

'I went along to see Doris with a friend,' said Erdal. 'She took us into the house and we sat down and I was expecting that she would concentrate and call something down. In fact it wasn't like that at all.

'I thought nothing was happening. Doris was just chatting to us and then suddenly she seemed to get onto the right frequency. She said she could hear a woman talking about a policeman.

'I couldn't think of any policeman in the family but Doris said the woman insisted that this particular policeman was a family member. I couldn't place him so we left it and she moved on, but about half an hour later when she was talking to my father the policeman was mentioned again. He was definitely in the family she said, and he was now on the other side. And then I remembered that my uncle, who died seven or eight years ago, had been a policeman!

'It was an extraordinary experience. Doris gave me my mother's name – an 'a' sound, she said, Ayse – the fact that she had died in her sleep and hadn't been able to say goodbye and that she had five children and six grandchildren. All correct.

'She said my mother told her that four of her five children had got married and were happy but for a while she was worried about me because I hadn't settled down. I was the last of her children to marry but she was pleased now because I'd married a good wife and we were having a baby.

'She told me that I had my mother's wedding-ring. Not the ring she was given when she married but a more expensive ring my father had given her years later when he'd made his money. (This was true. I kept it at the time in my safe.) She said my mother wanted me to give the ring to my wife when she'd had the baby.

'She also gave me my father's name and the fact that he'd died suddenly of a heart attack. All correct. Then she turned to my friend and said, "There is someone interrupting. It's your father. He died of cancer and he suffered for three months. You weren't there when he died. His name is Abba."

'My companion was very shocked indeed. He hadn't been expecting any messages for himself but, once again, Doris was absolutely right.

'She went on to talk about the boat and the island – incidentally I've since bought the boat from my brother and I've changed the name to Ayse so I hope my mother is happy now! – and my brother Nail who deals with money and book-keeping (correct) and my sister who is having problems with her nerves at the moment (also correct). She also said that my sister moved house just after my mother passed away. I thought she moved before my mother passed away but when I discussed it with my wife later she reminded me that it was in fact after, so Doris was correct again!

'Finally, she said she could see a long bay with a very nice beach and a beautiful sea. This is where we have bought some land and at the moment we are building a hotel there.

'There were many other family details, including a brother who died twenty-two years ago when he was only twenty-one, but these were the things that most stand out in my mind. I was amazed by the whole experience. I do believe in life after death but I felt very nervous at the beginning of the sitting.

'The night before, I prayed to God and asked that it would work because I badly wanted to know if my parents and my brother had met and were together. I know that my prayers were accepted because Doris gave me the details I needed. Afterwards I felt much better. It was a very great relief.'

Erdal was pleased with his sitting, that was clear, and he has kept in touch ever since. I was the first person he telephoned when his little daughter was born.

'Has my mother said anything about the baby?' he asked me.

I tuned in and immediately I heard Mrs Danyal's

voice. 'It's a girl and they've named her for me,' she said proudly.

'You've named her Ayse after your mother,' I told Erdal and he confirmed that this was true. His mother was thrilled and I expect she'll watch over her little granddaughter with special care.

Obviously, as I explained. I was unable to see baby Ayse in hospital, but Erdal and his wife Filiz invited John and I to tea a few weeks later. We had a lovely afternoon.

It was the first day of the big freeze of January '87, but Erdal sent a car to collect us and we were driven in comfort through a shivering London to a luxury apartment block in Kensington. There we sat on the ninth floor looking out over the snowfields of Kensington Gardens, eating delicious Turkish pastries made by Filiz, and drinking tea.

Ayse was asleep when we arrived but by the time we'd finished our first cup, she was awake and ready for inspection. Filiz put her into my arms, a warm little bundle in a deep blue babygrow, with velvety brown eyes and a cap of dark hair. She was absolutely gorgeous.

John, who'd rather overdone it that morning shovelling snow off the path and had consequently been feeling groggy ever since, perked up tremendously at the sight of the baby and insisted that he had a cuddle too.

All in all it was a special afternoon. It brought back memories, too. Erdal had employed a nanny to help Filiz with the baby while they were in England and watching her bob about in her dark dress and black stockings I was instantly reminded of my own nannying career. I was also fascinated to learn how things have changed since my day.

Ayse was suffering a little from wind.

'Oh, you'd better give her a drop of gripe-water,' I remarked automatically to the nanny.

'We haven't got any,' she said.

'Haven't got any? Oh, I suppose you've run out.'

'No, we don't use it,' said the nanny. 'There's no point. The doctor says it doesn't do any good at all.'

I was amazed. When I was a nanny we used to swear by gripe-water. No nursery was complete without it.

'No good?' I said. 'But in my day we used it all the time.'

The girl shook her head. 'Well we don't any more. The doctor says you might just as well give the baby plain water.'

I could hardly believe it. The doctor must know what he's talking about of course but to think of the gallons of gripe-water we must have poured down our babies for nothing! Surely it wasn't just our imagination that the little mites felt better after their 'medicine'.

I was also surprised at the way modern nannies swing a baby on to their shoulder. The girl was very careful of course, but in my day we never moved a child without cradling its head in one hand. It's much more casual now.

'This is how they teach us to do it now, Doris,' said the nanny with a smile as she patted Ayse's back and carried her away.

I don't know, I thought to myself, if I was trying to be a nanny in this day and age they'd think I was dreadfully old-fashioned. I'd better stick to being a medium.

Mind you, I don't regret my nannying years. I enjoyed them tremendously at the time and it certainly opened my eyes to the very different ideas of motherhood held by some women.

Loving children as I have always done, I couldn't imagine anything more wonderful than having a baby of my own and spending every possible moment with it. What's more, I believed that every woman naturally felt the same way – until I became a nanny myself and came across many different sorts of mother.

Some were busy women who didn't have the time to be with their children every minute of the day. Some were in poor health and couldn't cope with a boisterous child; others just needed a bit of help, but a few it must be said, simply weren't cut out to be mothers at all.

These were the women who would hand the baby over to the nanny on every possible occasion and appeared to take very little interest in it at all.

I remember one woman I worked for who asked me to do her a special favour and work on Sunday, my day off. It was the baby's christening, she said, and she couldn't manage without help.

Well, John wasn't very pleased because we valued the one day a week we could spend together as a family, but I couldn't refuse.

'Well, all right,' I said reluctantly, 'but I can't stay late.'

'No, of course not, Mrs Stokes. I quite understand, and my husband will run you home afterwards.'

It was a grand affair. Guests arrived from miles around in large shiny cars, the women resplendent in bright hats and matching coats, the men smart in well-cut suits. I felt quite shabby beside them and I kept in the background while the service was conducted and the proud mother posed for photographs.

Then to my surprise, when the last camera was put away, the baby was thrust into my arms.

'We'll see you back at the house then, Mrs Stokes,' said my employer and off she went with her friends, leaving me to change the baby, settle him back in his pram and wheel him slowly home.

Soon a magnificent garden party was under way and baby was forgotten. I fed him, changed him again and put him down in his cot for a nap, just as I did every other day. Perhaps I was wrong, but I got the impression that his mother was more interested in her guests than in her son.

It seemed strange to me at the time but it was good experience. Quickly I learned that we're all different and those early lessons helped me understand the plight of the penniless young girls you get nowadays, stranded alone in a tower block with a baby. I expect some of them are temperamentally unsuited to motherhood but, unable to afford a nanny, they have to struggle along as best they can. Is it any wonder that sometimes they can't cope?

The cold days of winter brought another delightful meeting. At around the time of our afternoon with the Danyals, John and I were invited to tea with our Indian friend, Sam.

For years Sam had only been a voice on the phone. As I think I explained in one of my earlier books, Sam first became interested in spiritualism when he was working for the Indian Embassy in Germany. Waiting for a telephone call in the office one day he found himself listening to the radio which was tuned to the

World Service and as luck would have it the programme was about my book.

As the interview went on, Sam grew so interested that, afterwards, he telephoned the publishers and asked them to send him a copy. Then tragedy struck. Three weeks after receiving the book his little daughter passed over. It was a terrible, terrible blow, but later when he got over the shock Sam contacted me to let me know how much my book had helped him in his grief. He has been phoning ever since.

On one occasion I happened to say: 'And how's your wife? Is she feeling a little better now?'

'Well, yes, I think so,' said Sam, 'though she still misses our daughter very badly of course.'

But before he'd even finished speaking I heard another voice telling me the good news.

'Don't worry, Sam,' I said firmly, 'your little boy is on his way.'

Sam was astonished. He wanted to believe me but he found it very difficult.

'Really, Doris?'

'That's what they've just told me,' I assured him. 'And they're never wrong. I make mistakes sometimes but they don't.'

Sam went away cheered but incredulous. Unknown to him however, his wife had an appointment with the doctor the next day and that day it was confirmed that she was pregnant. Their son, Manfred, was born several months later.

In recent years Sam has been able to visit me a couple of times when he's been posted to Britain, but 1987 was special. Not only was Sam himself in Britain, but his parents were visiting him here too.

'Do you think you and John could come over for a

cup of tea?' asked Sam. 'My parents would love to meet you before they go back to India. They've read all your books.'

So once again, John and I found ourselves driving across London on a cold afternoon for a warm welcome and an exotic tea.

Oddly enough, we discovered that Sam was renting a house in Dulwich on the very same estate where Margaret Thatcher has bought a retirement home. It made me smile to think that having grown up with Margaret Roberts, as she then was, in Grantham, and having seen the corner shop where she started, I should now get the chance to see the place where she was planning to end her career.

The car brought us to an elegant estate where large mock-Georgian houses looked out over wide, open-plan lawns. There wasn't a wall or a hedge to be seen until we turned into a private side-street and suddenly came upon a place that positively bristled with fences. It was the future Thatcher home.

Very nice inside, I'm sure, although I was surprised at how close together the houses had been built.

Once again we had a lovely afternoon. Sam's wife served us with tea Indian-style, made with hot milk, accompanied by delicious apple pancakes, apple flan and yoghurt sweets.

Afterwards, Manfred, now grown into a quiet, beautifully-mannered little boy, played happily with the belated Christmas present we'd brought him – a radio-controlled car, while we adults chatted about every subject under the sun including reincarnation.

The time raced by and I think we were all sorry when it was time for John and I to go home.

I must say, moan though I sometimes do about

overwork, I'd hate to have to give up my job. You really do meet the nicest people when you're a medium.

Chapter Five

It was Christmas Day. The tree was glowing softly in the corner, the radio was playing carols and the house was filled with the smell of roasting turkey.

Happily, I started picking up discarded wrapping-paper before Boots could chew it to bits. Boots, of course, thought it was a marvellous game and trotted after me making little darts at the screwed-up sheets.

'Don't you dare!' I said, pretending to scold, as we had a fierce tug of war over one holly-strewn piece. 'I'll have your guts for garters if you get that all over the place.'

It was quite a tussle but Boots eventually conceded defeat, and just as I straightened up, the phone rang.

'Hello! Merry Christmas!' I said, stuffing the paper under one arm.

'Hello,' whispered a shy little voice, 'I'm going to sing.'

And she did: 'We wish you a merry Christmas, we wish you a merry Christmas, we wish you a merry Christmas and a ...'

The paper fell from my arms and I stood there listening to the song with tears stinging my eyes. Little Beverley George was no Aled Jones but that carol was the most beautiful sound I heard all Christmas.

They'd said there was no hope for Beverley. At just a few weeks old she had suffered such a savage beating she was left blind, crippled and brain-damaged. She was a cabbage, her foster-mother, Wendy, was told and unlikely to live beyond a year.

Yet thanks to Wendy's faith, courage and devotion, Beverley, now nine years old, could see, talk and enjoy life.

'Thank you for my walking-frame,' said Beverley when she'd finished the song. 'I love you.'

'It's a pleasure, darling,' I croaked round the lump in my throat. 'You're worth it.'

We'd never met Beverley in person but John and I have known about her for a long time. She is a very special little girl. When she was about eighteen months old her foster-mother had written to us in despair. An orthopaedic surgeon had just told her:

'We don't waste our time on handicapped children.'

Now I'm not suggesting for one minute that this is the general attitude of orthopaedic surgeons, but this particular man was obviously tactless to say the least and he upset Wendy very much.

'I've got no one else to turn to,' she wrote to us. 'The surgeon says there's nothing that can be done, but I can't just give up on Beverley. I'd be very grateful if John would put her on his healing list.'

At this stage the child couldn't lift her head or move her legs and the medical profession held out no hope.

It seemed terrible to us to write off a poor little mite like that, and besides, John turns no one away. Beverley went on his absent healing list that very day.

Absent healing can't guarantee a cure, I must stress.

If it's your time to pass over there's nothing that will hold you back. But healing will ease suffering, smooth a passing and in some cases, result in a dramatic improvement or even a cure.

What's more, in Beverley's case, contrary to what the doctors said, I felt that there was a lot of hope. Not for any medical reason (I'm not a doctor after all) but because quite clearly, the spirit world was hard at work on the child's behalf.

Already a couple of strange things had happened. On Christmas Day, when she was just one year old, Beverley had suddenly and quite unexpectedly got her sight back. Wendy had been warned that the little girl would probably never see again, yet on Christmas morning, she looked directly at the bright glass balls on the Christmas tree and reached out for them.

Tests revealed that the action wasn't just a coincidence. Beverley could definitely see.

It was like a miracle for the Georges but there were still serious problems. Beverley also suffered from terrible fits, sometimes undergoing ten or fifteen a day. In order to minimize the damage they caused and keep them under control, she was prescribed a number of powerful drugs. There was no alternative to medication, Wendy was told.

Mrs George struggled on somehow and that year she even managed to take Beverley away on holiday to Wales. One afternoon, as they were sitting on the promenade enjoying the sunshine, a strange thing happened.

'A woman suddenly approached us,' said Wendy. 'I'd never seen her before in my life. She could have known nothing about Beverley or what was wrong with her and yet she came up to us and said: "You are killing that little blossom bud. The more you give her those drugs, the more she will shrivel up and die." As she spoke, she cupped her hands into a bud shape and crumpled them. "But the more you take her off the drugs," she continued, "the more she will blossom and bloom," and she opened her hands like a flower unfurling. Then she walked away and I never saw her again.'

Wendy was naturally taken aback. There was something about the woman's manner that impressed her. She could not just dismiss her words and yet she felt confused and unsure. After all, the woman had not mentioned any kind of medical background that might lead her to give this advice and what she was suggesting could be very dangerous indeed.

What's more, Wendy, who was devoted to Beverley and had done everything in her power to help her, rather resented being told that she was killing her foster-daughter, albeit with kindness.

And yet, and yet … How had the woman known that Beverley was on drugs in the first place? It seemed very odd. And there was something about her manner … Wendy couldn't put her finger on it but she had the strangest feeling that she ought to take the woman's advice.

I believe that the woman was sent with a message from the spirit world. She might even have been a spirit person. But Wendy, of course, who knew nothing of such things at this time, simply found the incident oddly disturbing.

Nevertheless, by the time she got back to her room she had decided that she would be mad to do anything but stick to her doctor's conventional advice. And who can blame her? But that night Beverley suffered a terrible fit.

Wendy was badly shaken. She had given the child the correct dose of the prescribed medicine and yet it had done nothing to prevent the fit. If the drugs were not doing her any good and might possibly be doing her harm, then Wendy decided she didn't want anything more to do with them.

'But when I suggested this to the doctor she was furious,' Wendy recalled. 'She wanted to know why I was doubting her advice. After all, I had no medical training and she had spent years learning about such things.'

It was a difficult situation but the more Wendy thought about it the more convinced she became that the strange woman was right and the doctor was wrong. The next day she stopped Beverley's drugs.

'And she hasn't had a fit since,' said Wendy.

The years passed, Beverley slowly improved and Wendy kept us in touch with her progress. From being a helpless little rag doll, unable even to lift her head, Beverley changed into a cheerful, chattering child who could crawl about the house by dragging herself along with her arms. She was able to go to a special school in a wheelchair and she could enjoy the company of other children. No one could call her a cabbage and the experts were amazed.

We hadn't heard from Wendy for a while and so one day, when we were leaving for Birmingham where I was to appear at the Odeon, I must admit that I didn't give her a thought. It didn't even cross my mind that Wendy lived in a little village not too far from the city.

Still, when we arrived at the hotel there was a letter waiting for me in Wendy's hand-writing and as I

66

read it, I could have kicked myself.

'Oh, John, what a shame,' I said. 'If only we'd thought. Wendy says that she tried to get tickets for herself and Beverley to come to the Odeon but they were sold out. If only we'd realized we could have asked Laurie to save her some.'

It was too late to organize anything now. It's very difficult for Wendy to do things at a moment's notice. Instead, we had to be content with a phone call.

'Oh, what a shame,' I said again as I unpacked my case. 'I would have loved to meet Beverley.'

John dialled the Georges' number and had a good old chat with Wendy. Then when he was fully up to date with Beverley's progress, he passed the phone to me.

'What a pity, love,' I said. 'If only we'd known before. We would have loved to see you.'

'Never mind, Doris,' said Wendy. 'Maybe next time.'

I didn't answer. She must have thought me strange, but at that precise moment someone from the other side butted in. Oh no, that can't be right, I thought, but I had to blurt it out just the same.

'You haven't had a baby today have you, love?' I asked, though I felt sure she wouldn't be talking to me on the phone like this if she had.

'No!' squeaked Wendy in amazement.

'Well, someone in your family has,' I persisted.

I think it was the grandmother who'd arrived to tell me the good news. She didn't stay long but she was quite definite.

'Actually my sister has,' said Wendy slowly.

'That's it,' I said relieved. I wasn't going barmy after all. 'A little girl.'

'Yes, that's right,' said Wendy.

'And she's got the name the wrong way round!' said the grandmother, but not crossly.

'Got the name the wrong way round?' I queried silently. 'What d'you mean, love?'

But grandmother was hurrying off somewhere, probably back to the baby and she didn't have time to chat.

'Just tell her. She'll know,' she said, as she moved away. 'She's got the name the wrong way round.'

And then she was gone.

'Well I don't understand this,' I said to Wendy, 'but I'm sure your nan just said that your sister's got the name round the wrong way.'

Wendy gasped. Then she started to laugh. 'Yes! Yes, she would. The baby's called Charlotte Elizabeth and Nan's name was Elizabeth Charlotte!'

Good old Nan, I thought. She doesn't miss a thing. Still, I'm sure she appreciated the fact that the baby was given her name even if it was in reverse order.

I hadn't intended to get into a sitting and it was only a tiny scrap of information, yet I hoped it would make up to Wendy for missing the demonstration. I started to 'switch off' but before I did so I picked up an agitated vibration from Wendy. She was worried about something.

'Is anything wrong, love?' I asked 'You seem a bit bothered about something.'

'Well, yes, I suppose I am, Doris,' Wendy admitted reluctantly. 'Not bothered so much as angry, really.'

It turned out that she'd heard about a wonderful invention that could mean a lot to Beverley. It was a special sort of walking-frame in which a child like Beverley could be strapped upright, her feet on a swivelling platform which would move when she moved her shoulders. A twitch to the right would swivel the feet to the right, a twitch to the left would turn the feet in that direction and gradually the child would 'walk' across the room.

'Beverley's never been able to stand upright,' said Wendy, 'and it's her dearest wish to help me with the washing-up. This frame would allow her to do that. It would make her feel she was walking and it would strengthen her legs which are like matchsticks.'

There was only one problem. The frame cost much more than the Georges could manage and the council wouldn't help. Apparently they lived in one area but Beverley went to school in another and each authority said the other should pay. Wendy was left feeling that she was asking for some unreasonable luxury.

'Well, John,' I said, when Wendy had finished pouring out the sad tale. 'What shall we do about this? I think we'd better help. All right, Wendy. Don't worry about it. The money will be in the post.'

Wendy was flabbergasted. She had had no thought in her mind of asking for financial help from us – she'd simply poured out her troubles to a friendly ear.

'Oh, Doris … I don't know what to say,' she stammered, 'I wasn't hinting … I mean …'

'I know, love,' I said, 'but it will be a great pleasure for us to help. After all, a girl of nine should be able to stand up and walk if she possibly can. It's not a luxury.'

Wendy was thrilled. I couldn't stand chatting for long because I had to get ready to go to the theatre but I think our short conversation made her day.

It turned out to be a marvellous day for me, too. Readers of my earlier books will remember the time when I worked as a nanny for Wyn, the lady who lived in the big house near us in Grantham and who taught me how to lay a table properly, which fork to use and all manner of useful things. Well, Wyn has long since passed over, but her husband, Stan, now a fine old gentleman of eighty-six, is still going strong and he was coming to see me on stage for the first time, that night.

I had another special guest too. Rusty Lee, the irrepressible TV cook, had agreed to come on stage and introduce me. I'd met Rusty a few years earlier when we were both invited to be in the audience of Dame Edna Everidge's Celebrity Night Out on the South Bank.

Rusty walked into the room, a bouncing bundle of undiluted energy with a 100 kilowatt smile. She took one look at me, rushed over and threw her arms round my neck in a great big hug.

'Oh, I've been longing to meet you,' she cried and she chattered away and roared with uninhibited laughter for the rest of the evening. She was truly a sunny personality. She brightened a room just by walking into it.

Rusty moved to Birmingham shortly after this and one day, while driving past the Odeon, she saw my name on a poster outside. When she got home she phoned to see if she could get a ticket but they were sold out. Undaunted she asked to speak to the manager.

'Well, Rusty,' said the manager when she explained the problem, 'come down and we'll see if we can fix you up.'

Rusty duly arrived with a great big bouquet of flowers and the manager squeezed her into the theatre somehow.

'Oh, Rusty,' I said, when I saw her later in the dressing-room,' I don't suppose you've been very comfortable.'

'I've been fine,' she insisted, 'I'm having a wonderful time.'

'Well, I'll tell you what,' I said. 'Next time I'm at the Odeon why don't you come up on stage with me? We'll definitely find you a chair – you can be chairman for the evening!'

'I'll hold you to that, Doris,' grinned Rusty. 'I'd love to.'

She was as good as her word. And that night when I arrived at the Odeon, there she was, smile as wide as ever, eager to begin.

Stan arrived shortly afterwards. It was a bitterly cold night for anyone to turn out and Stan, who had to walk with the aid of two sticks, must have found it more difficult than most, but he came beaming into the dressing-room with the lady who'd brought him.

'I'm so proud of you, Nanny,' he said. 'You do Grantham proud.'

Then he stopped. 'Oh dear. I must remember to call you Doris, but somehow it just comes out as Nanny. I know. Supposing I called you Poll?'

Long before I worked as a nanny, my nickname as a child had been Polly, or Poll for short.

'That's all right, Stan,' I said. 'As long as it's polite I don't mind what you call me!'

And I sat him down and gave him a cup of tea and a sandwich to warm him up before the demonstration began.

I didn't know whether I was coming or going that night with the excitement of my visitors and the crowded dressing-room. Hardly had we got Stan settled in his place of honour in the theatre than it was time for Rusty and I to go on stage. I just about managed to pat my hair into place and straighten my dress and I was on.

Rusty didn't seem a bit nervous. She strode out and chatted to the crowd as if it was composed of one or two old friends and not a theatre full of strangers. She was a great asset to the atmosphere. When there was an amusing moment she roared with laughter and set the entire audience off. When there was a touching moment I looked round and saw that there were tears pouring down her face.

Stan had his moment of glory too. I explained to members of the audience who hadn't read my books, about Wyn and all the things she'd taught me.

'That was a very long time ago, of course,' I said, 'but tonight I'm very thrilled because her husband is here in the audience. Come on, Stan. Stand up.'

And Stan, still an elegant man despite his age, stood up proudly and took a bow. The audience gave him a wonderful round of applause and he sat down again almost scarlet with pleasure.

It was pretty hectic during the intermission in my dressing-room. Rusty was in fine form, handing round cups of tea and making everybody weak with laughter at her jokes. It was great fun, but after a while, I realized I needed to tune in in order to sort out some contacts for the second half and I couldn't do it with all this noise.

Quietly I slipped into the bathroom to escape the hilarity. I stood there at the mirror fiddling with my hair and trying to concentrate.

'Poo!' said a spirit voice.

Slightly offended, I sniffed the air. 'There's no smell

in here,' I told my unseen critic indignantly. 'Not unless you mean my perfume, and I think it's rather nice.'

There was a merry laugh.

'Not poo. Pugh!' she repeated. 'My name is Pugh and my husband is here. He was the last but one contact.'

Quickly I replayed the first half in my mind and I remembered an extremely thin man with dark hair and very intense dark eyes. He'd come up to the microphone because I'd made a contact for him but unfortunately I lost it almost immediately and most of the messages turned out to be for other people.

I do my best but this often happens, I'm sorry to say. Spirit people frequently think that because I can hear them, their loved ones can suddenly hear them too, and so almost as soon as they get through to me, they go darting over to their relatives or friends to talk to them and I lose them. They move off the vibration and another spirit person comes forward to take their place.

'I would like to speak to my husband,' said Mrs Pugh. 'Will you try again?'

'I'll do my best, love,' I promised her, 'but we always start the second half with question time. Will you wait around till that's over?'

'Of course,' said Mrs Pugh.

Sure enough, this time we got it right. Mr Pugh came back to the microphone and his wife talked to him at length about the children and how much she missed them. Poor girl, she'd suffered very badly and she'd left behind her a beautiful baby.

As she talked about it, Mrs Pugh showed me a mental picture of her bedroom. Her husband was in bed and he was cuddling something in his arms.

'Do you cuddle a pillow in bed at night?' I asked him.

'No,' said Mr Pugh.

'Well, she's giving me an impression of being in bed and I've got something in my arms and I'm cuddling it,' I said.

'That's the baby,' said Mr Pugh. 'Ever since my wife went, I've slept with the baby. I go to sleep with my arms round her.'

He had been devastated by his wife's tragic passing but now he felt a tremendous sense of relief to know that she wasn't totally lost.

All in all, I had a very happy time in Birmingham and though it was hard work I knew that the effort wasn't in vain. Come Christmas I received a beautiful letter from Mr Pugh, enclosing a photograph of the baby.

'Becky has quite taken to you, Doris,' he wrote, 'and calls you her new granny.'

I also heard from Beverley in the nicest possible way. Apparently these days she's getting on wonderfully with her walking-frame. She scoots about the house and classroom, she's learning to read, she's about to start learning to write and, best of all as far as she's concerned, she's helped her mum with the washing-up.

'The first time, she got water everywhere,' said Wendy. 'The kitchen was flooded. But I wouldn't have cared if the whole house was awash. I just stood there and watched her with tears in my eyes. I never thought it would be possible. It was like a miracle.'

And just to round off a very special Christmas, we went to a pantomime.

Apparently Lewisham Theatre, where I do so many demonstrations I'm almost part of the family, was putting on *Snow White and the Seven Dwarfs* starring Gary Wilmott, that year. We hadn't been planning to go but Chris Hare, the manager, phoned and invited us.

'It's a good show, Doris,' he said. 'You'll love it.'

Now I must confess to a weakness for pantomimes. I know they're not everyone's cup of tea but then maybe I'm a child at heart. Anyway, I knew I'd love it too and I wasn't disappointed.

Chris met us at the door and made a great fuss of us. He took our coats and put them in his office for safe keeping, then he escorted us to our seats. It was the first time I'd seen the theatre from that side of the stage and I was impressed.

The seats were a pretty pink and very comfortable and there was plenty of leg-room. Even better still, though it's not a service everyone gets, I realize, as soon as the curtain came down for the intermission, Chris arrived with two cups of tea for us. We felt thoroughly spoiled.

Almost as soon as we arrived a hand tapped me on the shoulder and a woman said: 'Excuse me. It's Doris Stokes, isn't it?'

'Yes love.'

'Don't you want anyone to know you're here?'

'I'm not bothered, love,' I told her.

She began rummaging about in her handbag. 'In that case,' she said, 'would you mind signing an autograph? It's a new book and you'll be the first one.'

Naturally, people saw what was going on and a few minutes later I had a little stack of programmes and odds and ends to sign. But people were very good.

75

They didn't pester us and we were able to enjoy the show in peace.

And it was just as well I hadn't been hoping to make a visit incognito because even before the curtain rose, a voice announced:

'Tonight, ladies and gentlemen, we've got Doris Stokes in the audience, so if you want to know how the story ends, you'll have to ask her.'

Marvellous though Gary Wilmott, who played a page called Muddles, was, I think it's children who make a show like that and the kids were hilarious that night.

When Snow White collapsed after eating the fatal apple, the dwarfs came home unsuspecting from their work and stomped about the cottage saying: 'Why isn't our supper ready?'

Then they discovered Snow White's body.

'She won't wake up, what's the matter with her?' they cried in distress.

'She's bloody well dead!' answered a boy behind me.

A bit later on, the Dame accidentally lost his wig and another small boy in the front row leapt to the stage, shouting in glee: 'You're a man! You're a man!'

The wig wasn't the only mishap that occurred that night. For reasons that escape me now, there was a camel involved in the plot – a pantomime camel, that is, played by two men, one at each end – and at one point the creature's udders fell off and you could see this man's arm groping around the floor for them.

'They're over there! They're over there!' yelled the lad in the front row.

He was so excited that at every point in the story he rushed to the edge of the stage to join in the conversation with the characters.

'You're mad,' he told Gary Wilmott after Muddles the page did something particularly daft. And without warning, Gary leaned down from the stage, picked him up and swung him high in the air.

'If I have any more trouble from you …!' he threatened jokingly.

The boy loved it. He was giggling so much he could hardly stand upright when Gary put him back on his feet again.

Naturally, when volunteers for a children's band were requested, our little friend from the front row was there first.

'What's your name?' Gary asked him.

'Richard,' said the boy.

'I might have known,' said Gary. 'Tricky Dicky.'

The instruments were handed out and surprise, surprise, there was an instrument for every child but Richard. One had a tambourine, one had a horn and one had a recorder but there was nothing for Richard.

'Oh. We haven't got anything for you,' Gary told him.

But the audience was sighing, 'Ahhhh.'

So, reluctantly, Gary went into the wings and came back with an enormous drum.

Well, Richard had a field-day. He really went to town on this drum. He boomed round and round the stage until Gary said, 'All right, all right. Don't take over the show.'

It was hilarious and by the end of the evening I was hoarse from shouting: 'Oh no, it isn't!' 'Oh yes, it is!' and all the rest of the daft things you do when you're at a pantomime.

Afterwards Chris brought us our coats and led us

backstage to meet Gary.

What a nice boy he was. There was no sitting about drinking in his dressing-room for him. He'd changed into his street clothes ready to go straight home to his family.

'I saw you on *This Is Your Life*, Gary,' I said when we were introduced. 'What a lovely little girl you've got.'

'Yes. That's Katie,' he said proudly. 'She's two now and we're having another one in two weeks' time!'

This was his first pantomime, he explained, and he'd been very nervous about it, but the rest of the cast had been a great help to him. He was enjoying it immensely.

'And of course the kids in the audience make the show,' he added.

Well, they'd certainly done him proud that night.

John and I went home with sore throats from shouting and aching faces and sides from laughing so much. Just the result you'd expect from a thoroughly good pantomime!

Chapter Six

It was the moment millions of us had been waiting for. The glittering carriage stopped outside Westminster Abbey and Sarah Ferguson climbed elegantly onto the pavement, taking care not to crumple the foaming ivory skirts of her dress.

She looked beautiful and the wedding dress, about which there had been so much speculation, was truly magnificent.

'Oh, John,' I said, wallowing happily in sentiment. 'I think that's the loveliest dress I've ever seen.'

Sarah Ferguson and the newly-created Duke of York made a handsome couple and I felt sure they were well suited. Sarah seemed a brave, bright girl, able to cope sensibly with the pressures of royal life and she was old enough to know her own mind. As for Prince Andrew, I'm sure he had been much in love with his former girlfriend Koo Stark but he would never have married her. Sarah was different. Sarah was his friend. Andrew and Sarah were clearly mates in every sense of the word and that's an excellent basis for marriage.

I don't think I moved from the television set all day. The real life events were more fascinating than any soap opera as far as I was concerned. But then perhaps that was because I had a special reason to be interested. I felt almost personally involved, because just the night before I'd been celebrating the happy event at the Cafe Royal at a glamorous pre-wedding charity ball packed with celebrities and beautiful people.

Now, I'm not much of a one for going out. I don't drink, I can't dance much with my shaky leg and I'm getting on a bit after all, but the Royal Wedding Ball was different. This was a really special occasion and I wouldn't have missed it for the world.

I was having a little holiday at our chalet on the coast when the invitation arrived. Funnily enough I woke up that morning with an old song going round in my head:

'Give yourself a pat on the back, a pat on the back and say to yourself, jolly good health, you've had a good day today. Yesterday was full of trouble and sorrow, nobody knows what's going to happen tomorrow, but give yourself a pat on the back, a pat on the back and say to yourself, jolly good health, you've had a good day today.'

I hadn't heard that song for years and yet, as I stood there putting on my dressing-gown, I realized that someone from the spirit world was singing it to me.

I wonder why I'm being serenaded this morning, I thought, somewhat puzzled, as I went off to run my bath. And they weren't just sending me a song. Along with the music came a great feeling of anticipation, almost as if some nice little treat to cheer me up was on its way. Yet we weren't expecting any visitors or exciting events. The day ahead promised to be quiet, uneventful and relaxing.

'Well I don't know, John,' I said, over breakfast. 'They're still singing this song and yet we've got nothing planned at all.'

A moment later the phone rang. It was Terry. He'd stayed at home to look after Boots and the house and he tended to ring with daily bulletins on his progress.

Mentally I ran through the meals I'd left in the freezer for him.

'Hello, love,' I said, when John handed me the phone. 'Now there's a bit of chicken you could have for your dinner tonight, but you'd better get it out now to defrost … Or if you prefer, you could have …'

'Hang on a minute,' Terry interrupted. 'I didn't ring to talk about my supper. I've just been looking through the mail. Would you like to go to a charity do?'

'Not right now, Terry, we're on holiday.'

He laughed. 'So you don't want to go to the Royal Ball, then?'

'Royal Ball?' I asked. 'What Royal Ball?'

'They're having a pre-wedding ball at the Cafe Royal and you've been invited. If you'd like some complimentary tickets you have to fill in a form and send it off.'

I was thrilled. There would be no need to interrupt our holiday and it sounded like a tremendously exciting affair. I'd never been to a ball before.

'Of course I'd like to go, Terry!' I shrieked. 'Could you send off the form for us?'

'I've already done it!' he chuckled. 'I knew you wouldn't want to miss this.'

Well, I spent the next few weeks agonizing over a dress to wear. Since I'm not in the habit of going to balls, my wardrobe isn't exactly overflowing with ballgowns and in any case I wasn't even sure what they wore to do's like that. Still, after much asking of advice and hunting round, I found a smart, pretty dress which I was assured was just the thing. And after all, I told myself as I hung it in the wardrobe, even if it's not quite right, with all those celebrities around, no one will be looking at me.

The night before the wedding, John, Laurie, his wife Iris and I all presented ourselves at the Cafe Royal in good time. We put our coats in the cloak-room and walked into the ballroom where the sight made me gasp. The whole place was decorated to look like a summer garden and the girls, the beautiful girls in their ball-gowns, took my breath away. They were just like flowers blooming.

One of the girls on our table was really glamorous in an off-the-shoulder dress of gold lamé that went down into a train and swept the floor behind her. Another had tiny white roses in her hair, a white lace bow hanging down at the back and an exquisite white dress with a boned bodice smothered in little pink roses.

It was all terribly grand but everyone was very friendly and we had a wonderful time. There was a delicious meal with the most marvellous dessert which had been specially created for the wedding. It looked like a flower on the plate and when you dug your spoon into it, it was filled with strawberries.

After dinner the waiter brought round little carrier bags containing perfumes and soaps, party poppers and streamers and small Union Jacks. Then the band of the Coldstream Guards marched in and played a truly rousing selection of tunes: 'I'm Getting Married in the Morning', 'Congratulations', 'Rule Britannia', 'Land of Hope and Glory' ... and by the end of the performance we were standing up and waving our flags and singing along like mad. It was a marvellous experience.

Later on Leslie Crowther conducted a session of bingo and then there was a raffle for all sorts of gorgeous prizes from a holiday at the Hilton Hotel in New York, to a £150 necklace. It was all in aid of country holidays for deprived children and the prizes had been donated by the guests.

John and I had given a cheque and a camera. We didn't win anything but then we didn't expect to. We had a wonderful time. Leslie Crowther came up and personally thanked us for our gifts, as did Lord and Lady Arran, and we chatted to quite a few celebrities. Lenny Fenton, who plays Dr Legg in *EastEnders*, brought his wife over to our table to say hello. June Whitfield, who was looking very young and lovely, passed by close enough to touch. We saw Tony Blackburn and Paul Daniels and as we were leaving at about 1.30 in the morning we met Ray Allen standing outside the door.

'Hello, Doris,' he said. 'Have you come out to get away from the noise?' Because by now the place was vibrating to loud pop music, the young things were dancing away and to be honest you couldn't hear a thing anyone was saying.

'No, we're off home now. We're not night birds,' I told him. 'Mind you, it is a bit loud, isn't it!'

The young people looked set to go on all night but John and I were very glad to get back to our beds. Besides, we wanted to see the wedding the next day and if we stayed out much longer I knew we'd be good for nothing in the morning.

As it turned out, we were yawning quite a bit but

we arrived at our stations in front of the television bright and early for the royal wedding. Somehow, having attended the ball made it all seem more personal. The fact that we'd been drinking the young couple's health the night before made us feel almost like invited guests.

I love weddings at the best of times but royal weddings are something special. All that colour and pageantry – even the most cynical of men can't help getting drawn into it.

'Oh, I'm sure they'll be happy,' I said to John as we toasted Andrew and Sarah once more in tea. But this was just an emotional wish, not a prediction. As I've explained before, I'm not a fortune teller. Very occasionally a spirit person will give me a tiny glimpse ahead in the life of a sitter, but most of the time I know about as much of what's in store in the future as the next person – that is, nothing.

And sadly for many people, the marriage that starts off so full of hope and happiness in a wonderful wedding, ends not long afterwards in tragedy.

This was brought home to me very forcibly around royal wedding time by two quite unexpected occurrences.

The first happened one afternoon when I was alone in the house. John had popped out to the shops, Terry was off seeing to something and I was struggling round with my shaky leg trying to do all the housework because Jean was on holiday.

I was half-way through the dusting when the doorbell rang.

'Oh dear, I suppose John's forgotten his key again,' I said to myself as I went to answer it.

But it wasn't John. I found myself looking into the

wide, tragic eyes of a very young girl.

'I'm awfully sorry. You'll think I've got a terrible cheek ringing your bell,' she blurted out before I could say a word, 'but I wrote you a letter last week and I hadn't heard and ...'

'Well dear, all my letters go to the office first,' I explained, 'and quite often it's a few weeks before I even see them. I'll give you the office number, shall I ...'

I stopped. There was something in her face, such a deep despair that I knew I couldn't send her away without talking to her.

'You're in great trouble, love, aren't you?'

Tears welled up immediately in her eyes.

'Yes,' she whispered, swallowing hard. 'But I didn't mean to come. I don't know what made me. I was on my way to my sister's but I found myself outside your door.'

'Well, come on in and have a cup of tea,' I said. 'But you must understand I can't do a sitting for you. There are so many people waiting now that I get into terrible trouble if someone jumps the queue.'

'Yes, of course. I quite understand.' said the girl. 'But I'd better get my baby. I've left her in the car.'

She ran up the garden path and came back with the most adorable little girl, no more than eighteen months old, in her arms.

'This is Hayley,' she said.

We went inside and Hayley sat quietly while her mother and I had a cup of tea. It turned out that the poor girl had lost her husband just a month before and she didn't know which way to turn.

'I queued up for two and a half hours to get tickets for your demonstration at Lewisham,' she explained, 'but somehow I couldn't wait. I don't know what to do with myself ... I didn't mean to come, I really didn't but I just sort of ended up here ...'

I did my best to comfort her with the hope that her husband would be first in the queue at Lewisham but even as I was speaking I realized that her husband had arrived. He was in the room with us and it would have been cruel to ignore him.

I couldn't do a proper sitting because it would have caused such problems (life isn't simple any more) but I was able to give the girl a few little scraps that cheered her up. Her husband told me the whole sad story.

Apparently they had been on holiday in Spain with his two little boys from a previous marriage. Everything had been fine. They were having a very happy time and one morning the husband got up to make breakfast for them all. He had seemed perfectly fit and well but without warning he just collapsed and died as he was preparing the meal.

Unknown to them all he must have had something wrong with his heart and it chose that moment to give out.

The poor girl, still reeling with shock, had to get herself, the children and the body back to England and see to all the arrangements.

It was a terrible, terrible thing to happen.

The husband who was still quite upset to have been so suddenly parted from his family and his earthly life, wanted his wife to know that he still loved them all and was still looking after them from the other side.

'You will tell her,' he begged me.

'Of course I will, love,' I promised.

'He says he still loves you all very much,' I repeated out loud to the girl, 'and he's watching over you. If ever you need him just put out your hand and he'll be there.'

It wasn't a proper sitting, of course, but by the time she'd finished her tea, my unexpected visitor had dried her eyes and declared herself much better.

I thought at first that she was merely being polite, but not long afterwards she was back on my doorstep, bright and smiling, with a huge bunch of flowers. She looked a different girl.

'You don't know what you did for me, Doris,' she said, giving me a big hug. 'I was desperate but now the pain is easier ... I can sleep at nights now ...'

A few weeks later there was another desperate appeal. Laurie had a telephone call from one of the administrators at University College Hospital. Apparently they had a very sick young man on a life-support machine and all they could get out of his distraught wife was that she wanted to speak to Doris Stokes.

'I know Mrs Stokes is very busy,' said the administrator, 'but is there any chance that she could speak to this young woman?'

Laurie promised to ask me right away, which he did.

'Of course I'll talk to her,' I said when he explained the situation. 'I don't know whether it'll help but I'll do what I can.'

So Laurie called the administrator back and shortly afterwards the kind lady had got the whole family assembled in her office to talk to me on the phone.

It was very difficult. The poor family were extremely distressed and they were hoping against hope that the boy, whose name was Graham Monroe, could be saved. Yet when I tuned in I realized that he was half over already and that it wouldn't be long before he was completely in the spirit world.

In my mind's eye I saw a picture of a good-looking young man with red-streaked brown hair.

'Has he got auburn hair?' I asked. 'Or, at least, brown hair with reddish streaks?'

'His hair's brown,' sobbed his wife, 'the red is the blood. They haven't washed the blood out yet.'

I comforted her as best I could and promised that we would pray for Graham.

'John will put him on his healing list and we'll do everything we can,' I assured them. But privately I knew that no earthly power would keep that boy here because he already had one foot in the spirit world. The best we could hope for was that he would slip gently over without trouble or pain.

My heart went out to that grieving family and it was very difficult to sleep that night. I could imagine them gathered anxiously round the life-support machine trying to will their strength into a body from which the life had all but departed.

The next day, Pat, Mrs Monroe's mother, phoned to tell me they were leaving Graham on the life-support machine for one more day. But as I expected, there was no change. Graham showed no signs of life and on the third day she phoned again to tell me that they were going to switch the machine off.

I was very sorry for them but I knew they had made the right decision. Later that day I popped up to fetch something from my bedroom and half-way up the stairs I suddenly felt a tremendous sense of relief. It was as if a great weight had been lifted from me and I was floating light and free. I knew at once what had happened.

'Graham's safely over,' I called down to John who was busy at his absent healing. 'He won't need healing any more. He's fine now.'

Not long afterwards the Monroe family came to see me at the Palladium and when the show ended Graham's wife and her mother came backstage to say hello.

Graham was with us in an instant. He was a strong, athletic young man, full of health and vigour.

'Doris, I wouldn't have wanted to be a vegetable,' he said. 'Do tell them it was for the best. I couldn't have stood being a cabbage. I was always so active.'

And he poured out the whole story. Apparently he was a scaffolder and on this particular day he'd climbed up the ladder and stepped onto a board that wasn't secured properly. The plank tipped and he crashed down head first. He didn't stand a chance.

'I didn't want to come over,' he said bitterly. 'We'd only been married a year, the baby was only five weeks old and we'd just bought a bungalow to do up. I was so looking forward to it ... But if the accident had to happen I'm glad I came over here. I would have hated being in a wheelchair ...'

He sent a great deal of love to his wife and said that he wanted her to live a full and happy life. If she met someone else she could love, she wasn't to hesitate.

'I'd like her to marry again,' he said, 'I want her to be happy and I don't like to think of her on her own the rest of her life.'

Finally he asked her to give the baby a big hug for him.

It was another sad story and I must admit that I said goodbye to the Monroes with a heavy heart.

I don't know, I thought to myself, it's all brides and young widows at the moment. From the joy of the royal wedding to the grief of a young wife and mother left alone to fend for her family.

Why do these things have to happen? I wish I had the answers. They say it's God's will but it seems a very harsh will to leave a young girl alone with a baby to bring up. No doubt the poor widows learn a great deal from their experience but it seems a terrible way to learn a lesson. Sometimes I get very confused with it all and I don't know what to say to the kids when they ask me why.

All I can say for certain is that I know a little of how they feel. During the war, John, who was a para-trooper, went missing at Arnhem and I was told that he was presumed dead. As far as the War Office was concerned, I was a widow.

Later, (as I explained in my first book, *Voices in My Ear*), the spirit world told me that John was in fact alive and would be coming home, but for a time I, too, believed I'd lost him. It was a dreadful blow and I've never forgotten it.

When you see the tragedy all around it makes you wonder why husbands and wives don't appreciate each other more and why we don't work harder at our marriages. I'm sure that far too many couples throw their marriages away, when in fact if only they'd tried, they could have saved them. It's a great shame.

These days I'm a bit old-fashioned and I believe that if you're married, you're married. Obviously if you've been unfortunate enough to marry a man who beats you or is cruel to the children, then of course you must get out as soon as possible. But in most other cases I believe that you should stick it out.

Marriage is like any other job. You have to work at it and it's not easy, as even Sarah Ferguson and Prince Andrew will find out in time. The trouble is, these days, with divorce being so easy, far too many people seem to give up when the problems begin.

I don't blame them. I know just what it's like because I walked out on John once and if it hadn't been for the good sense of my mother, who knows, I might be a divorcee by now. But thank goodness I listened to her, because if I hadn't I would have missed years of laughter and tears, years of sharing and loving – a whole lifetime of precious memories. What a waste that would have been.

It seems so long ago now, but the trouble began when John came back from the war. I knew he had been wounded but I had no idea of the extent of his wounds, and neither had he. He had suffered severe head injuries and was left with a hole in the back of his head, but the hair had grown over it and no one would have realized it was there.

When he was sent back from the prison camp an army doctor gave him a quick examination and pronounced him unfit for further service. The head injuries weren't even noticed and John was too confused and disorientated to point them out.

All I knew when he came home was that he seemed a different person. The man I married had been a big, strong, athletic type with medals for boxing and football. The man who came back was quiet and withdrawn and couldn't even walk around the house without bumping into things, let alone play football.

I didn't understand what was wrong so I nagged. John was frightened because he himself couldn't understand what was wrong, so he lost his temper. All in all, after the initial euphoria of his homecoming had worn off, we had a miserable time.

Then one day after a row, I decided I'd had enough. I packed my things, slammed out of the house and went round to my mother's.

'I've come home,' I said, dumping my suitcase on the doorstep.

Mum stood in the doorway eyeing the case sourly. She didn't move aside to let me pass.

'Well you can just get yourself back again,' she said, blocking up the doorway even though she was a tiny little creature.

She was nothing if not blunt, my mum. She hadn't approved of my marrying John, but now I was married, then married I should stay.

'You've made your bed, now you must lie on it. You just get yourself back and cook that man's tea.'

I was pretty put out I can tell you. 'You would have thought you could expect some sympathy from your own mother,' I muttered angrily as I trudged away, my case getting heavier and heavier with every step.

I didn't want to go back but I had too much pride to go round to a friend's house and risk the possibility of being turned away again. There was nothing for it but to go home and make up the quarrel.

And make it up we did. There were more quarrels of course but knowing that I couldn't run home to my mother made me stand my ground and gave me added incentive to make the marriage work. It wasn't easy, but after two years we finally got some proper medical treatment for John and discovered what was wrong.

John was sent to Stoke Mandeville Hospital for a

while. The treatment helped him and gradually he came to terms with his disabilities. I'm not saying there was an overnight miracle, but after that things grew easier and easier and I knew that our marriage was safe.

We've been together now for well over forty years – living proof that you can make a marriage work if you try hard enough!

Chapter Seven

Friday, March 6th was a dreary day. The weather was cold and dull and by evening a steady rain had set in. Outside, the crocuses were flowering well but the day belonged more to winter than to spring.

And so it was on that wet, gloomy evening that we first heard the news of a disaster that shocked the world.

John and I, supper over, had just settled down with a pot of tea to watch television. But the set had hardly warmed up when our programme was suddenly interrupted by a newsflash.

The teacups froze in our hands as we listened in horror. A Townsend Thoresen ferry, the *Herald of Free Enterprise*, had capsized just outside Zeebrugge. Hundreds of passengers were on board and every boat in the area was racing to the rescue.

Like most people, I think, our first reaction was one of total disbelief. I'd never been on one of those ferries but I'd seen pictures of them often enough. Huge and solid, seemingly crammed to overflowing with cars and excited holiday-makers, they looked stable, well-made and indestructible. How could one of these giants possibly turn over in a calm sea before it had even properly left the harbour? It just didn't make sense.

Yet, believe it or not, as that tense evening went on, it became clear that if anything the tragedy had at first been underplayed. Hundreds of people were saved, of course, but as we discovered later, close on 200 were killed.

Those poor souls, I thought. I've always been a bit claustrophobic and the idea of being trapped in a ship as it rolled over in the water made me shudder. How did they bear it? Even the ones who returned safely must have gone through an appalling ordeal.

What a way to end a holiday. My mind went back to my last stay in hospital. While I was there a number of nurses were collecting coupons for just such a trip. Apparently, a national newspaper was offering shopping-trips on the continent for £1 plus a number of special coupons printed in the paper. Every morning when I'd finished reading the news, I shared my coupons amongst the eager nurses.

I could only pray that I hadn't unwittingly sent some poor young girl to a watery grave by my choice of reading material.

For days afterwards, accounts of the disaster and the complicated business of recovering bodies went on and the newspapers were full of harrowing tales. Then in the midst of it all, Laurie rang. A desperate couple who'd lost their son in the tragedy had contacted him. Naturally, they were distraught and they wondered if I could help.

'What d'you think, Doris?' asked Laurie 'I know you're very busy.'

I didn't hesitate. There was no question in my mind. I knew I had to see them. 'Fit them in somehow, Laurie,' I said. 'I'll see them as soon as I possibly can. In the meantime, I'll give them a ring.'

Mrs Reynolds had been in quite a state, as any mother would have been. Her son, Jonathan, and his fiancée, Fiona, had set off for a day's shopping-trip to Belgium, planning to return aboard the ill-fated *Herald of Free Enterprise*. They never came back. Since then Fiona's body had been recovered but Jonathan's was still missing.

There was no doubt in my mind. Jonathan was definitely on the other side. As I talked to his parents on the phone a young man's voice suddenly chimed in on the conversation. I had Mrs Reynolds in one ear and Jonathan in the other. He gave me a few family names. His mother was called Joan, he said, his father was Alan and his sister was Sonya.

'They feel bad because my body is still trapped down there,' he said, 'but tell them not to grieve. It doesn't matter at all because I'm not under the water. I'm here and I'm safe.'

I passed this on to Alan and Joan and I tried to explain that a body is just a coat we put on when we come to this earth and that once our time here is done, we don't need it any more. It really doesn't matter what happens to our old clothes. A funeral is just a comfort for the living – it serves no useful purpose to the loved one who's gone on, although he may well attend because it's a big family gathering, just as he'll attend future weddings, christenings and celebrations, because he's part of the family.

By the end of the conversation they seemed calmer and I think the chat brought them a little comfort.

Shortly afterwards they came down from their home near Oxford for a full-scale sitting. I'm sorry to say that when they arrived at midday I was still in my dressing-gown and not at all sure that I could go through with it. Once again I seemed to have been struck down by some mysterious complaint. My head ached. I felt dizzy every time I tried to stand and I kept going hot and cold. To make matters worse, we had a blocked drain that day and workmen were bustling backwards and forwards and the phone kept ringing.

Laurie called early that morning to drop in some papers and he found me weak and ready to panic.

'I don't think I'm going to be able to manage, Laurie,' I said anxiously 'I feel so rotten I think we'd better change it to another day.'

But when Laurie rang the Reynolds' number there was no reply. They'd already left.

'Oh well,' I said as philosophically as I could, 'we can't turn them away. I'll just have to hope the spirit world doesn't let me down,' and I swallowed a couple of Disprin and crossed my fingers.

I'm so glad now that I did. The three Reynolds arrived dressed in black. They were smart and composed but the tension around their eyes belied the calm exterior. Inside they were suffering badly.

Laurie showed them into the front room and brought them coffee while I apologized for my dishevelled appearance.

'I'm so sorry,' I explained, 'I haven't been at all well and it was all I could do to get out of bed this morning. I don't know if I'm going to be any good to you.'

'That's all right, Doris,' said Mrs Reynolds sympathetically 'We quite understand. We're just glad you could see us at all.'

'Well, I can't promise anything,' I warned, 'I'll do the very best I can but quite honestly I don't know if it's going to work.'

97

'Well, if it doesn't, it doesn't,' said Mrs Reynolds reassuringly.

We sipped our coffee and chatted about the weather and the journey and the problems with the drains and all the time I prodded with my mind at the spirit world. At first there was a great deal of confusion. Hardly surprising really, when you consider how many poor souls found themselves ejected without warning into the spirit world in such an unforeseen tragedy.

Then, through the confusion there came a great sense of urgency. There was some important news on the way. In fact the news should be arriving that very day.

'I think we're ready now,' I said at last to the Reynolds. 'I'm getting a feeling of confusion and then this urgency. Something about some news. Have you had some news today?'

The family shook their heads.

'No,' they said.

'Well, there's some news on its way and it could come today,' I said.

They shrugged. There was, after all, no way of telling if I was right or wrong. Yet later that evening when I turned on the television, I was just in time to catch an announcement that the date for the attempted refloating of the *Herald of Free Enterprise* had been fixed that very day. The refloating was an important event because without it the remaining bodies could not be recovered.

This was the news the spirit world had been preparing us for. As it turned out, the intended date came and went and the ship stayed where it was, due to bad weather, but, nevertheless, the message had been correct. There was news that day.

That out of the way, two bright young people stepped boldly into the picture. I could hear them laughing and chattering together for several moments before they moved close enough to speak to me. What a happy pair they sounded. I've never heard a couple laugh so much as these two.

'Shush a minute, Fee,' said Jonathan, 'I just want to tell them we're together. They've been worrying about that. They think we got separated but we didn't. We came over together and we're going to go on together from now on.'

All three Reynolds were visibly relieved when I told them this.

'Thank goodness,' whispered Joan Reynolds almost silently, eyes half closed.

And suddenly I understood her fears. Fiona's body and the body of her thirteen-year-old sister, Heidi, had been found while Jonathan's had not, and she was worried that because they had not been 'laid to rest' together they might be separated for all time.

Of course, it doesn't work like that at all. People who both want to be together, can be together. They meet up as soon as they pass over if they wish to, it's as simple as that, but Joan, Alan and Sonya weren't to know.

'Now, I know we don't want to dwell on it,' I said silently to Jonathan, 'but can you tell us what happened?'

'There were seven of us,' he explained.

Later the Reynolds confirmed that Jonathan, Fiona and Heidi had indeed been part of a party of seven who'd set off on a day's shopping-trip in Belgium – just for the fun of it.

'Fiona and I went to the bar to get a drink,' Jonathan went on, 'and we got separated from the others. We never saw them again ...'

As his words died away I felt the dreadful sensation of icy water all around me and a terrible dark, confined space. The water crept higher and higher and I could hear people screaming.

Quickly I closed my mind to the impression. With my claustrophobic tendencies I couldn't take much of scenes like that.

'It's okay, Jonathan, I get the picture,' I told him silently, 'Don't dwell on it, love.'

'I could swim and I was trying to help people ...' Jonathan went on, 'but there was no way out.'

A bit later, he came in too close to me and I could feel my lungs filling up with water. I began choking and gasping for air.

'Jonathan!' I called out mentally. I didn't have enough breath to say it aloud. 'You've come in too close. Move back a bit, love.'

This sometimes happens with inexperienced spirit communicators, especially if the medium is tired or below par generally. The medium loses concentration and unintentionally fails to remind the spirit person to keep a safe distance between them. When this happens the spirit person's last impressions come across so strongly that the medium starts to live them, with potentially dangerous results.

Once I'd finished coughing I felt it was wiser to stick to more mundane subjects. I asked Jonathan if he'd had anything of value on him which his family could keep when the body was eventually found.

'A watch or something,' I suggested.

I felt him shake his head. 'Not really. My watch

wasn't very safe,' he said.

'That's right, he was talking to me about it not long ago,' said Joan. 'The metal bracelet was dodgy.'

Jonathan gave some more family names and details and then I got a number. Someone lived at twenty-something. It was very fuzzy. Could have been twenty-two.

'Fiona lived at twenty-seven,' said Joan.

And at the mention of her name, Fiona made Jonathan stand aside for a moment to let her speak.

'All my things are still there at number twenty-seven, just the way they were,' she said. 'Tell them not to grieve. You see, my parents were separated and for a while it was difficult for me. Jonathan was my life. I wasn't very happy before I met him but then we met and he was everything to me. I looked on his parents as my parents and I loved them very much.'

'You'd better!' interrupted Jonathan, teasingly.

And then they were laughing again.

'Come on, you two!' I said, pretending to be irritated as the giggles went on. 'Let's give your mum and dad a bit more to go on. What did you do for a living, Jonathan?'

Instantly I was given a picture of a table piled high with books and papers and sheets of writing. It looked very much like a student's untidy desk.

'Was he studying?' I asked the Reynolds. 'Because he's showing me lots of books and papers. Was he still at college?'

'Yes, he was,' said Alan.

It turned out that Jonathan was only nineteen years old and he was taking a course in surveying and land management at a polytechnic.

Jonathan's rich, dark brown voice came back. He

101

really did have a beautiful voice. Call it fanciful, if you like, but some voices sound light blue to me, yap, yap, yapping gratingly on the ear. But Jonathan's voice was warm and deep. A real dark brown, and a pleasure to listen to.

'I really got down to my studying when I met Fee,' he said. 'I was determined to make a good life for her. And I would have passed my exams, you know.'

But sadly, he wasn't given the opportunity to prove himself. Nevertheless he was a talented boy and his talents weren't going to waste. Now and again I could hear piano and guitar music in the background and this was Jonathan's way of telling me that he played those instruments on the other side.

'Very likely,' said Joan, when I told her what I could hear. 'He used to play the piano years ago and recently he started playing the guitar.'

We hadn't heard much about Alan during all this and I felt it was time to bring Mr Reynolds into the conversation.

'What does your dad do, love?' I asked Jonathan.

Immediately, a picture of ladders leapt into my mind.

'He's always up and down ladders,' said Jonathan. 'Buildings and things.'

'Yes, that's right,' said Joan, 'Alan's a builder.'

Then I heard the name Laurence.

'That's our accountant,' said Joan. 'He was sorting out Jonathan's account.'

'Then there's Julie.'

'That's my friend,' said Joan.

'And now he's talking about Spain,' I went on. 'Are you going to Spain?'

'They had a holiday in Spain a couple of years ago,'

said Joan.

'No, what I'm trying to say is that I don't want them to think that their life has got to come to a stop,' said Jonathan. 'I want them to have a holiday, to go to Spain or wherever. Don't you agree, Fee?'

Fiona agreed.

I was getting tired by now but Jonathan hadn't quite finished. He turned towards his sister, Sonya, a quiet girl with blonde hair, wearing an elegant black dress, and said something about a new car or a blue car. It was difficult to tell which.

'Both are right!' said Sonya in delight. 'I've got a new blue car.'

'And who's Trish?'

'Oh God,' said Sonya, laughing nervously, 'she's a friend I should have picked up today but I forgot!'

'See, I know what she's up to!' laughed Jonathan.

Before he went, Jonathan even found time to remember the dog.

'She's got a growth, you know and it's time she came over here with us. Don't let her suffer,' he said.

'Yes, she has. She'll be with him soon,' said Joan.

The power was rapidly draining now and the young people began to move away but before he went, Jonathan said impishly:

'Oh, one thing more before I go. My mother,' – I thought he said mother but it turned out to be his father – 'didn't like my name abbreviated. It always had to be Jonathan, but everyone else called me Jon and that's how I signed my name. So I want to say, Jon and Fee send their love!'

That set them giggling again and the last I heard was the sound of merry laughter as the couple returned to their life in the spirit world.

But that wasn't the last I heard of Jon and Fee. Shortly afterwards I spoke to the Reynolds on the phone and they told me that many of the names they'd been unable to place during the sitting had since made sense to them.

'For instance,' said Joan, 'there was a Harold or Harry. Well, we couldn't think of anyone of that name at the time, but afterwards we remembered a Salvation Army Major we'd met in Zeebrugge who was very kind to us. His name was Harold.

'Then, when you were talking to Fiona you mentioned Barbara and Carol and also something about a photo album. It didn't mean anything at the time but when we got home we looked through the photo album and there was a picture of Fiona with her friends Barbara and Carol.'

This often happens so I wasn't surprised. People attend sittings in an emotional state and it's very difficult to remember every relative, friend and acquaintance at a time like that. It's only afterwards that the significance dawns. So no, I wasn't surprised, but I was glad that the Reynolds were pleased with that morning's work.

The weeks went by and the *Herald of Free Enterprise* continued to make the headlines. The operation to right the ship was hampered at every turn by the weather and the date seemed to be changed and changed again. Then one morning while Laurie and I were discussing some office work and the ferry disaster was far from our minds, I suddenly heard Jonathan's voice. The letter I was reading slipped from my hand, so great was my surprise.

'Sorry to interrupt,' said Jonathan, 'but I just wanted you to tell Mum and Dad that my body's been found … Oh, and there's a service at Canterbury Cathedral for all of us who came over … I'll let you get on now.' And he was gone.

'Laurie,' I said slowly, 'Have you got the Reynolds' number? Could you give them a ring? There's been a message from Jonathan.'

Laurie spoke to Alan who was polite but puzzled. So far they'd heard nothing. Then a few hours later, he called back. They'd just heard. Jonathan's body had been found that day.

The service at Canterbury Cathedral took place shortly afterwards.

There's another little postscript to this story. A few days after Jonathan's funeral Mrs Reynolds was taken ill. It was during the night and there was a bit of a commotion but, surprisingly, their only grandchild, Nicola, normally a light sleeper, did not stir.

The next morning Alan remarked on her nice long sleep.

'Oh no, I wasn't asleep,' said Nicola. 'Jon and Fee came to play and cuddle me. They were with me for ages. It was lovely.'

Some people would have said it was a dream, but the child was so convinced the visit had really happened that Alan found himself believing it.

There's no question in my mind. Of course it happened. Knowing that their mother needed a bit of help, Jon and Fee kept the little one occupied until the drama was over. Any loving son and daughter-in-law would have done the same.

But I wasn't quite finished with the *Herald of Free Enterprise*. Not long after the Reynolds' sitting, another anguished couple, the Harrisons from Somerset, got in touch. They too had lost a son in the disaster.

aster.

Young Stuart, only seventeen years old, had been one of the token-collectors. He had saved up his coupons for a cheap day in Zeebrugge and it had cost him very dear.

Like the Reynolds, the Harrisons also had a grown-up daughter, and Karen accompanied them to the sitting.

Stuart was a lovely boy with sandy, fair hair which kept falling across his nose. When the ship turned over, he said, he'd tried to hold up a drowning child but they got separated and he was swept away. He remembered nothing more until he found himself in the spirit world.

It was another very sad story. Throughout the sitting Stuart kept going to Mr Harrison as if to try to comfort him, but this made it rather difficult to catch what he was saying.

I heard the name Andy.

'That's me,' said Mr Harrison.

'That's funny,' I said, 'I thought I heard him call you John.'

Mr Harrison laughed. 'Well, yes. My name is John but everyone calls me Andy.'

Like Jonathan, Stuart gave the names of family and friends and many other details. One point in particular stands out in my mind.

'Karen's going to get engaged, you know,' Stuart confided.

But when I passed this on, Karen blushed and shrugged her shoulders.

'Oh, I don't know about that,' she said.

'Well, Stuart seems pretty certain about it.'

Karen giggled and the matter dropped.

That night however, when she got home, her boyfriend proposed to her and she accepted. So now she's engaged just as her brother predicted.

I breathed a sigh of relief when I heard the news. How nice to have one happy ending to such a tragic story.

Chapter Eight

I could see the similarity as soon as I opened the door. The woman was svelte and beautifully groomed with immaculate hair and rich, dark eyes, but when she smiled, her face lit up and I saw her daughter, Benazir Bhutto, the brave child of the late Prime Minister of Pakistan.

In my last book, *Voices of Love*, I described how Benazir came to see me because she badly needed the advice of her father. He, poor man, had been hanged by the military regime and his son had died in mysterious circumstances. Nevertheless, despite the decimation of her family, Benazir was determined to go into politics and take over where her father had left off.

She knew, of course, that this was a dangerous mission, but her father promised that he would stand by her. The people would be on her side, he predicted, and she would return to Pakistan to a tumultuous welcome.

Well, everything he said came to pass. A few weeks after the sitting I turned on the television to see some incredible pictures of little Benazir, hardly more than a child to me, moving through the streets of Pakistan surrounded by a quarter of a million cheering people.

It was an extraordinary sight and I had to admire

Two views of Wembley Conference Centre, August 1986.
(*Above*) Enjoying a cup of tea in the interval backstage in the Green Room.
(*Below*) The audience I faced out front!

Six-year-old Collette Gallacher – 'A sunny, happy little soul arrived singing happy birthday in a sweet, childish voice.'

(*above*) Giving little Ayse Danyal a cuddle on a cold January day.
(*below*) Another cuddle, this time at a signing session in Birmingham.
Pugh brought his daughter along to see me after I had given him a spirit message from his wife at the Birmingham Odeon demonstration.

John, forty years to the day he came home from the war.

(*Above*) Jonathan Reynolds and his fiancée, Fiona Pinnells. Victims of the
Zeebrugge ferry disaster, they are now happy together in the spirit world.
(*Below*) Stuart Harrison, also a victim of the ferry tragedy. At a sitting with his
family he told me his sister was going to get engaged. And he was right!

Happy scenes from the magical trip on the Orient Express. *(Photographs courtesy of Steve Rapport)*
(Top left) Pete Murray was there.
(Bottom left) Opening one of the many gifts I received.
(Top right) Lillian Monger with John and me. Lillian's husband, John, made contact with her at the Wembley demonstration in August.
(Bottom right) The irrepressible Rusty Lee had John and me and Jenni Barnett from TV-am in stitches!

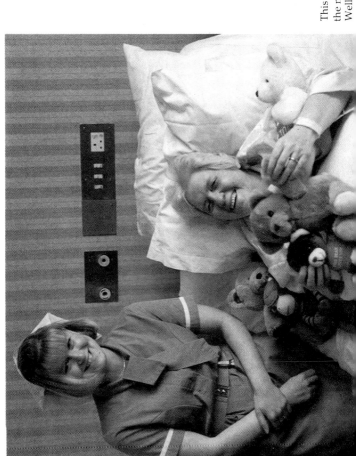

This happy photograph was taken on the morning of Doris' operation in the Wellington Hospital by her manager,

the girl's courage. During the sitting, I could hardly believe it when ex-Prime Minister Bhutto told me that his daughter, this quiet, self-possessed child, intended to rule Pakistan one day. Now, watching her triumphant return, I could not only believe it, I felt sure she'd eventually pull it off.

But Benazir's plans did not go smoothly. As the weeks passed, President Zia grew more and more alarmed by her popularity and at last he could stand it no longer. He had her arrested and thrown into gaol.

It was at this point that Benazir's frantic mother got in touch. She had already lost half her family in the cause of Pakistan and she was terrified that she was about to lose her daughter the same way. After all, if Zia could execute the Prime Minister without any serious repercussions, what wouldn't he do to a slip of a girl? She was desperate to know what advice her husband would give, and whether he had any message for Benazir.

'She'll listen to you, Doris,' she assured me, 'and I think I can get a message through.'

It seemed that Benazir was being treated reasonably well in prison, although for two days and two nights after she was arrested she was given no bed or bedding and had to sleep on the floor. She was more comfortable now but her mother feared what might happen next.

'Well, you must come at once, love,' I told Mrs Bhutto. 'This is a very urgent case.'

She arrived, outwardly as calm and self-possessed as her daughter but inside I knew she was shaking.

'Come in and sit down, love, and we'll see what we can do,' I said.

In fact, I had no difficulty contacting her husband.

He knew me already, of course, and having communicated before he found it easier the second time. What's more, he had a particular reason for wanting to speak to his wife at that moment. He, too, was very anxious about Benazir.

'Eleven days,' he said in the beautiful English that I remembered from our last chat. 'She will be freed in eleven days.'

'I don't know about that,' said Mrs Bhutto doubtfully. 'We haven't heard anything.'

I checked that I hadn't misheard but Bhutto was adamant.

'Well he seems to think it will be eleven days,' I assured his wife, 'but he's anxious.'

'She will go straight to Lahore when she gets out and this she must not do,' said Benazir's father. 'Tell her to lie quiet for a while. Let things cool down. She must go softly softly now.

'You see, at first Zia laughed. He thought she was just a woman and he didn't take her seriously. He takes her seriously now.'

Mrs Bhutto nodded unhappily. You could tell that she was heartily sick of politics and would like nothing better than to have her daughter return to Europe, get married and settle down to rearing a family like other women. She would sooner have grandchildren round her knee than a country at her daughter's feet.

Her husband obviously read her thoughts. 'The trouble is, Benazir's a lot like me,' he said. 'I would never climb down from a decision even if it meant my death. And my wife, whom I love dearly, understood this. I could have run away. They would have given me anything I wanted, but I could not do that.'

'Yes, I know,' sighed Mrs Bhutto, 'I would rather he had resigned and left everything, but he wouldn't.

The ex-Prime Minister moved closer to her so that it was difficult to catch his next words.

'I wonder now whether it was worth my family's happiness,' he said heavily, 'but much as I loved them all, I could not have done any different.'

Mrs Bhutto nodded again, 'Yes, that's true. He believed so much in what he was doing.'

Her husband was silent for a while, possibly regretting this sad state of affairs, but then his anxiety for Benazir forced him to speak out again.

'I'm afraid for my daughter because she is like me,' he went on. 'People are very fickle. At the time I was killed, the people were for Zia. Now they are for my daughter. I ask myself, is it worth the agony? Inside she is weeping but nothing will change her.'

He gave his wife the names of people she could trust – necessary advice at such a treacherous time for Benazir. Then he couldn't help harping back on his own abrupt execution. He was still bitter about that and refused to call it an execution at all. He would only say that he was killed.

'I never expected to be killed, you know,' he said. 'And it was at night. That is the way this man fights. Not in the daylight where people can see. I thought God would see me through but, looking back now, I wonder if I had gone into exile whether things would have been different.'

He was silent again for a moment, and then there came a great wave of love for his wife.

'I was so proud of her,' he said. 'She had carried this great burden yet she walked out with her head held high. My wife could have crawled, but she didn't.

111

She walked out like a queen.'

He remembered their forthcoming wedding anniversary and then went on to talk of family matters and his grandchildren.

By the end of the sitting I must say I'd grown heartily sick of the turbulent politics of Pakistan and I couldn't resist putting in my own two-pennyworth.

'Speaking as an ordinary person, love,' I said. 'I'd be tempted to say to hell with Pakistan, after all you've been through.'

Mrs Bhutto fished a crisp handkerchief from her bag. 'I know, I know,' she sighed. 'It's not as if Benazir couldn't do anything else. She could get a wonderful job anywhere with all her degrees. She's such a clever girl, but ...'

I nodded, 'I know. You can't change them. People like Benazir have something burning in them and there's nothing you can do.'

As we walked to the door, where Mrs Bhutto's car was waiting, her husband's voice came back like an echo ... 'Eleven days ...' but I didn't repeat it again. It seemed too good to be true and this woman had been through enough. I didn't want to raise her hopes only to have them dashed once again.

Yet, as usual, I should have trusted the spirit world. Eleven days later came the surprise news that Benazir had been released at 8.45 that day. Her mother of course was elated and I'm quite sure she passed my messages on.

Whether Benazir heeds her father's warning of course is another matter. I haven't heard much about her for a while now, so I can only hope that she's treading softly as her father advised. In the meantime I'm keeping my fingers crossed.

A few months after Mrs Bhutto's visit, I had another famous guest trying out the sofa in my front room. Eddie Large, that hilarious funny man from the *Little and Large Show* drove all the way from Bristol and back, just to spend the afternoon with us.

What a nice man he is. Like Freddie Starr, there was no side to him. He was natural and friendly, no airs and graces at all.

The visit came about through a newspaper article. I'm a bit of a newspaper addict, I must admit. Every day I look through most of the papers and the stories often prod me into spur-of-the-moment action. I've sent money to needy children, given a home to an abandoned dog (Boots) and taken an occasional editor to task, all because of stories I've read in the paper. So one day when I came across a sad article about Eddie Large, I found my hand straying automatically to the telephone.

Apparently, Eddie had been feeling very bad because he wasn't able to be with his parents when they died. He was torturing himself with guilt and in an attempt to find some comfort he had bought two of my books to see if they would help.

Now an awful lot of people who don't know about the spirit world suffer in the same way and it's such a shame because there's no need. Our parents know we love them. They understand the problems we face and it doesn't matter a bit to them who's standing around the bed as they pass over because they are concentrating on the people who've come to meet them from the spirit world.

These are long-lost loved ones whose sudden appearance fills them with wonder and joy. Once the parents are safely over they can come back and visit

113

their children whenever they wish and they know what the grieving family is going through.

It's all very simple. There's no need to say goodbye and no need to feel guilty. Yet people who don't understand this get themselves into a dreadful knot. I've seen the suffering it causes, and it made me particularly sad to think that Eddie Large was going through such agony, because he's given me so much pleasure over the years.

The times I've laughed till the tears ran down my face at his antics with Sid Little! If I could help him at all it would be the least I could do to repay him for all the fun.

I picked up the phone.

'Laurie,' I said when my manager answered. 'Have you seen this article about Eddie Large? It says he's bought a couple of my books because he's so distressed over the loss of his parents. Do you know his manager? I was wondering if you could tell him that if Eddie would like to talk to me, if there's any way I can help, I'd be glad to.'

'Okay, Doris,' said Laurie. 'I'll give him a ring.'

Not long afterwards the phone rang. I picked it up, thinking it was Laurie calling me back.

'Hello, Doris,' said a familiar voice. 'This is Eddie Large. I was wondering if I could come and see you.'

'Of course you can, love,' I told him. 'Any time you like.'

So a week or two later, John and I were running around with plates and sandwiches and bowls of salad and trying to make the table look pretty.

'What on earth are you doing all that for? You're daft,' said Terry, as he passed on his way to take Boots for a walk. 'You don't even know if Eddie'll be hungry.

114

He's only coming for a chat.'

'Well, you never know,' I said, squeezing a dish of tomatoes between a quiche and a plate of ham rolls. 'He's coming a long way. I expect the poor man will be worn out. He'll need something to eat.'

Terry raised his eyes in his 'the-old-girl's-barmy-but-it's-no-use-telling-her' expression.

'Come on, Boots. Let's get out of here,' he called, and he hurried away before he could be press-ganged into helping with the preparations.

I was still swopping plates around and wondering if there was enough food when there was a knock at the door and Eddie Large arrived. He was casually dressed in a leather jacket and woolly scarf and he looked exactly as he looks on television. I don't know why, but that's always a surprise.

'Come in, Eddie, you must be dying for a cup of tea after that journey,' I said, leading him into the sitting-room where the buffet was laid out.

His eyes opened wide at the sight of the food, 'Oh, Doris, I wasn't expecting all this.'

'Well, just help yourself, love. It's open house here.'

It took a bit of coaxing but Eddie loaded his plate, accepted a cup of tea and settled down for a chat. Like many comedians he was basically a quiet, thoughtful man and probably shy, deep down. The bubbly, extrovert nature only comes out when the spotlights are turned on.

I did my best to explain about the spirit world and what happens when you pass over.

'You see, you are never alone, Eddie,' I said, 'Someone always comes to meet you. That's why, if you've ever sat with people who're dying you often hear them talking to someone you can't see and who passed over years before. People say they're delirious. Not at all. They are seeing the spirit people who've come to meet them.'

Eddie listened attentively. He had just opened his mouth to ask a question, when suddenly I heard a woman's voice. 'That's right, Doris, you tell him,' she said encouragingly.

It was Eddie's mother – Jessie, I think her name was – and she was there in the room with us. After that, of course, the visit turned rapidly into a sitting. Both Eddie's parents came to talk to him and they were able to assure him that they understood why he couldn't be with them when they passed and that it didn't matter. When Jessie moved close I got an impression of glorious, red-gold auburn hair.

'Did your mother have auburn hair when she was younger, love?' I asked Eddie.

'Yes, she did,' said Eddie.

'Well, she's got it back again now. It's beautiful.'

What's more, Jessie told me that a child Eddie and his wife had lost through miscarriage was being cared for by herself and Eddie's dad.

'It's a little girl and she's got auburn hair, just like your mother's,' I went on. 'Oh, and your mother tells me February's important.'

'That's when the child should have been born,' said Eddie.

The sitting didn't go on all that long but, afterwards, Eddie assured me that he had found the visit comforting and that it was well worth the long journey.

'Where are you off to now?' I asked later, as Eddie, full of tea and salad and every other delicacy I could press on him, wound the woolly scarf round his neck once more.

'Oh, I'm going back to Bristol,' he said.

I was horrified. 'There and back in one day? It's too far, Eddie. Why don't you stay in London overnight?'

Eddie grinned. 'There's nothing to it, Doris. I do it all the time. I'm used to it. It doesn't bother me at all.'

And with a jaunty wave, he was away up the garden path, ready to tackle the long drive for the second time that day.

Not long afterwards, on Valentine's Day, I received a beautiful bouquet from Eddie. Inside was a little card: 'Thanks, Doris, for all the comfort you've given me.'

I was touched. I'd done so little. Just given a few hours of my time in return for so much entertainment.

The weeks passed, the weather grew warmer and all at once the bulbs in the garden were shooting into flower.

'Goodness, John,' I said one morning, as I turned over another page of the calendar. 'It's nearly April.'

Whenever I see April looming I think of my half-sister, Edna, whose birthday falls in that month, and this year I couldn't get her out of my mind.

'Edna will be sixty-nine this year,' I reminded John. 'Sixty-nine, nearly seventy. We really must get in touch.'

It's such a shame that we've drifted so much apart. We were never really close because our personalities are so different, but in recent years there has been no contact between us. I don't even have Edna's address. There hasn't been an argument, just a series of events that put greater and greater distance between us.

First Edna married a Catholic who disapproved of

spiritualism, and then they moved to Canada.

Well, neither of us has ever been much of a letter-writer and so out of touch did we become, that when I visited Canada a few years ago, Edna couldn't think who I was. I got her phone number from Directory Enquiries and as soon as I had a few minutes to myself, I rang her from my hotel room.

'Hello, Edna,' I said when she answered.

'Who is this?' asked Edna doubtfully. She didn't recognize my voice, that was for sure.

'It's Doris!' I explained. Well, after all these years I couldn't expect anything else. It was so long since Edna had heard my voice on the telephone.

But the name didn't seem to help.

'Doris?' said Edna, obviously doing a mental run-through of her friends and acquaintances. 'Doris who?'

I was taken aback.

'Your sister Doris. Have you forgotten you've got a half-sister?'

I shouldn't have been surprised. After all, as far as Edna knew, I was still tucked away in Lincolnshire. The last thing she expected was to pick up the phone and find her provincial little sister talking to her from the next city.

Once Edna got over the shock, we had a nice chat on the phone, but my schedule was too tight to allow a personal visit. Sadly, I left for England without meeting my sister.

We've always been chalk and cheese, Edna and I. She was small and blonde, while I was well built and dark haired. She was inclined to be squeamish whereas I tended to blunder in and get on with things.

When our mum passed over, poor old Edna couldn't face the funeral. She helped me prepare the food and cut any number of sandwiches, but when it actually came to the service, she couldn't bear it. She sat in the car round the corner until it was over.

Yes, we're as different as it's possible for two people to be, but we're sisters, and I think it's a shame that at our time of life we're not closer.

'You know what, John,' I said, as I went into the kitchen to put the kettle on, 'I really must write to Edna one of these days. It's daft to be so far apart when you get to our age.'

I'm sorry to say that I didn't get down to writing to Edna. I didn't have her new address, it would have taken a few phone calls to get it and, as usual, my attention was diverted by urgent matters which had to be attended to at once. Life is always like that, isn't it? There never seems to be enough time and, some-how, important but not pressing matters tend to get pushed aside.

I'm not complaining, though. I know I grumble at times but I enjoy my work. People often say to me:

'Doris, isn't it about time you retired? You're sixty-seven after all.'

But, you know, if you're a medium I don't think you can retire. Being a medium is not just a job. It really is a way of life. Several of my colleagues have passed over recently and though, like me, they were getting on a bit, every one of them was working till she dropped. That's the way it is with us mediums. We can't stop.

Actually, far from retiring, I took on another job this year – one that has given me enormous pleasure. I joined the staff of *Chat* magazine as a kind of spiritual agony aunt with my very own column. I was thrilled when the editor wrote to welcome me to the staff and apparently, within a day of the announcement being made, the letters came pouring in.

I even made a commercial for the magazine. *Chat* had employed an agency called Doxat, Chapman and Partners to make a television advert about my new column. The only trouble was, advertising regulations wouldn't allow them to mention it on screen. Apparently, advertisers aren't permitted to promote what is termed as 'superstitious activity'.

I'm not a bit superstitious myself and I certainly wouldn't call my work a superstitious activity, but there you are. It was no use arguing. Rules are rules after all and Mike Chapman from the agency had dreamed up a way round the problem. An actress was to run through the major features in the magazine for that week and then she was to turn to me:

'What else have we got, Doris?'

'This might take a long time, lovey ...' I was to reply, as if I could see into the future.

'You see, we can't mention the column, Doris,' said Mike, 'but we're associating you with *Chat* in the minds of the readers, which is the next best thing.'

It sounded fair enough to me and he obviously knew what he was doing.

'Okay, love,' I said. 'It doesn't seem too difficult to remember.'

The actress and I went to our positions, the lights blazed and the cameras started to roll.

'What else have we got, Doris?' asked the actress right on cue after the list of features had been read out.

'This might take some time, lovey ...' I replied

obediently.

'Smashing, Doris,' said the director, but I was too old a hand at television by now to imagine that I'd finished work for the day.

Sure enough:

'Could we just try that again?' he added, and off we went again and again and again. It's always like that with television. You need to be patient because you have to do everything about twenty times over.

After a few minutes, though, my concentration started to break up. The actress was saying her lines but suddenly I wasn't listening. Behind me I could sense the presence of a spirit person.

'I'm Tom,' said a man's voice. 'Tell her Tom's here.'

'Shhhh!' I said in my mind, 'I can't talk to you now. I'm making a commercial.'

The man ignored me 'But I must speak to her. Tell her it's Tom.'

'Look, Tom, I can't. You'll have to wait. They'll be furious with me here. Commercials cost a fortune to make. Every minute costs money.'

But Tom couldn't be bothered with such mundane matters as money. 'This is important,' he insisted.

'Later!' I hissed.

Quickly I glanced round to see if any of the crew had noticed my inattention and, to my horror, I realized they were all staring at me. I must have missed a cue.

'Everything all right, love?' said Mike, coming over ready to smooth out any problem. 'Getting tired?'

'No. No, I'm sorry,' I said, uncomfortably conscious that I was holding things up. 'It's just that someone keeps coming in from the other side.'

'It's that chippy!' said the director angrily. 'I knew

it. Right, I want everyone out from the back of the set. Now!'

There was the sound of footsteps and then a couple of bewildered young men appeared, unsure what they'd done wrong.

I couldn't help smiling. 'No, love, not the other side of the set,' I said, trying not to laugh. 'I meant the other side. The spirit world.'

There was an uncomfortable silence. Mike and the director exchanged looks. They obviously thought I was a nut-case. Oh well, in for a penny in for a pound, I thought.

'Does anyone here know someone called Tom?' I asked.

The silence continued. Then there was a scuffle in the shadows and a woman emerged, rather shyly.

'Tom's my uncle,' she said.

It turned out that she was the tea-lady and she'd been hanging round the studio ever since she'd heard that I was coming. She must have known intuitively that there would be a message for her.

'Well, he's come along wanting to talk to you, love,' I explained. 'Perhaps we can get together when I've finished here.'

The woman agreed to wait until the end of filming and, fortunately, this seemed to satisfy Tom too because once he heard what I said, he moved away and let me concentrate on my lines.

Things went smoothly from then on and the commercial was completed. Mike explained that they would have a lot of fun with special effects when they put the finishing touches to it and my voice would sound all echoey. I might even vanish at the end.

'You don't mind, do you, Doris?' he asked anxiously.

I think he was a bit afraid that I'd be all po-faced and silly about it. As it was, I just thought it was a great joke.

'Not at all,' I told him, 'I think it'll be hilarious. I can't wait to see it.'

Out of the corner of my eye I could see the tea-lady still hovering on the fringe of things.

'Come on then, love,' I called to her. 'Let's go and get a cup of tea and see if we can find out what Tom wants.'

Tom was back in an instant, of course, and there in the dressing-room I launched into a mini-sitting as I took off my make-up. It turned out that he was anxious to reassure his niece about some personal problems and once he'd done that he was happy to leave us all in peace.

It was great fun making the commercial, of course, but there's much more to being an agony aunt than larking around a television studio. I've always enjoyed reading the agony columns. Like many people, I turn to them first when I open a magazine. But I hadn't realized before what a responsible job it is. It suddenly hits you that people might actually follow the advice you suggest and for this reason the advice mustn't be lightly given.

I made up my mind to work very hard at each and every reply and I'm glad to say I've always stuck to that decision. Every week a very nice young writer called Nora McGrath arrives with a pile of letters and a tape-recorder, and then we sit down in front of the fire and work our way through them.

I read the letters and dictate a reply into the tape-recorder and then Nora sorts it all out afterwards at the office. The system seems to work well and there's never a shortage of correspondence.

Sometimes the readers confess to the most dreadful problems and when the subject is very complicated I often tune into the spirit world for guidance. Ramanov never fails me with his wisdom.

At other times the tone of the letters is so desperate that I feel compelled to phone the writer immediately and put his mind at rest. The answer still appears in the magazine a week or two later, but at least I know I've done my best. There are times when a week's delay can mean the difference between life and death.

There are many tragic letters, of course. Unless you do a job like mine you don't realize how much sadness there is in the world. But there are letters that make me laugh, too.

Not long ago a little girl from Nottingham wrote to me on the subject of reincarnation. She wanted to know if her granny had returned to her in the form of the family dog.

Well I roared with laughter when I read that letter, and in the spirit world I could hear her granny chuckling too. Nevertheless the child seriously wanted to know so, although I had to confess that the idea had made me smile, I explained that while I believed in reincarnation I didn't think her granny had come back as a dog.

'Animals have souls and they live on in the spirit world,' I said, 'but they're different from us. I don't believe for one moment that they can come back. They run free in the spirit world.'

The bulk of my letters, I suppose, concern worries that have grown out of all proportion in the minds of the writers. We find so many things to torture ourselves with, don't we?

Not long ago, two highly-distressed ladies wrote to me. One had been caught shop-lifting a few years before and was terrified that her husband in spirit knew about it and was so ashamed of her action that he'd ceased to love her.

The other, seriously ill with cancer, was desperate with guilt because after losing her husband she had launched into a couple of affairs, simply for the comfort of human contact. Now, facing the possibility of going to the spirit world herself, she was afraid that her husband would not be there to meet her because of her 'unfaithfulness'.

It's such a shame that these thoughts even have to cross our minds. I was able to reassure both ladies that they were still loved and respected as much as ever. Spirit people have a much better view of our problems than we do. They understand the pressures and strains we face and they don't condemn our actions.

Finally, now and again I get a really special letter. A letter so inspiring, so full of love and so unselfish, that it moves me to tears and I just have to share it with everybody. This next letter, reprinted with the kind permission of *Chat*, is just such a letter:

Dear Doris,

After ten years of longing for a baby my sister finally found she was pregnant. Her husband and she were thrilled beyond words. But tragically, their unborn son was lost at twenty-six weeks. From that cruel day on my husband and I couldn't stand to see their pain any longer. We decided to have a baby for them.

Don't misunderstand, Doris, because there is so much controversy about surrogate mothers, you may do. We gave her and her husband joy, we feel they deserve the baby I gave birth to this year.

I don't care what anyone on this earth says but I have to know; Doris, does my Nan approve? And does my sister's son know he has a little brother here?

We have two lovely boys who mean the world to us and we just wanted my sister and her husband to be as happy as we are.

Name and address withheld.

The tears trickled down my face when I read those words. How could she possibly think that anyone would disapprove of such a loving action? I could imagine so well the agony her poor sister must have gone through after losing her baby. It happened to me, after all, and how different my life might have been if a surrogate mother had been around to give me a child.

Of course, I know that there are all sorts of complicated problems surrounding surrogacy, particularly when it's done for money, but in a case like this I thought it was wonderful.

'My dear, what a wonderful, wonderful letter,' I wrote back, 'I'm in tears here. So much unselfish love that you had for your sister. You and your husband gave your sister the greatest gift that anyone in the world can give.

'Of course her son knows that he has a brother, and

126

he'll understand more when he's older. He's growing up in the spirit world.

'Your Nanna is over the moon that your sister has her own baby to cradle in her arms.

'Your gift of love has made everyone so happy. God bless you and your husband. I know you're all going to have very happy lives.'

I felt set up for the day after completing that case.

Yes, there's more to this agony-aunting than meets the eye, but I wouldn't miss it for the world. Long may the column continue!

Chapter Nine

Sadly, no matter how hard mediums work, there will always be sceptics; people who simply don't believe in life after death no matter what you say or do.

They dismiss my work and the work of people like me as trickery, telepathy or some kind of wicked spell.

Well, obviously, it hurts to be called a fraud, or worse still, in league with the Devil, especially when you work so hard to do good and to do your job well, but as I've said before, everyone's entitled to their own opinion. I don't try to force my beliefs on anyone and the doubters will eventually discover the truth for themselves on the day when, to their utter amazement, they wake up in the spirit world!

There is one area in the debate however where the sceptics are on shaky ground and that is the peculiar (to the doubters, not to me) phenomenon known as 'out-of-body experience'.

In recent years medical science has progressed so much that there are hundreds of people walking around today who have literally 'come back from the dead'. They have technically 'died' for a short time and then been resuscitated thanks to the efforts of hard-working doctors.

Now most of these people remember nothing of

the episode, but a striking number do, and although rather embarrassed because they fear no one will believe them, when pressed, tell of an extraordinary experience in which they felt they stepped outside their body and embarked on the start of a wonderful journey.

Often they can repeat word for word the conversation going on in the room when medical staff thought them unconscious or even dead.

But what has amazed and baffled doctors and scientists is that although the accounts they collected have come from all over the world and from people from all walks of life who have never met each other, the stories of the wonderful journey are almost identical. The details may differ, some may describe a river that formed the boundary with the spirit world, others a gate, but in practically every case the essential elements are the same – some sort of tunnel and a very bright light.

I know what these people are talking about because I, too, have shared this marvellous experience. Over thirty years ago I almost died after a fallopian pregnancy. Suddenly, in the midst of my pain, I saw my father and my son John Michael, now grown from a baby into a handsome little boy, standing hand in hand at the foot of my bed.

As I stared at them, the pain melted away and they started to move backwards. Somehow I followed them feet first into a glorious tunnel of bright, whirling colours, and at the end of the tunnel I could see a bright, bright light. Once I reached that light I knew I'd be in the spirit world and all my troubles would be over.

I was filled with a wonderful sense of peace and

love but it was not to be. Suddenly there was a great jolt, the tunnel, my father and son disappeared and I was back on the bed in hospital. The pain and the harsh, raw light of earth flooded over me and I was not at all happy to be back.

In common with all the other people who are privileged to undergo this experience, I have never been afraid of death since. I don't find it baffling. It makes perfect sense to me. You can't travel from one place to another without a journey in between, so when we pass from this life to the spirit world, we naturally embark on a journey quite unlike any other we have made.

To the scientists, however, many of whom don't believe in life after death, the out-of-body phenomenon is a difficult puzzle. They can't dismiss hundreds of ordinary people unconnected with each other as liars or frauds, as they can mediums.

So there can only be two explanations. Either these people really did go on a journey as they described or they were suffering from some kind of hallucination produced by a dying brain.

The scientists tend to prefer the hallucination theory. Now, I'm not clever and I don't have any technical education, but this explanation seems a bit strange to me. Is it likely that every dying brain in the world is programmed to produce an identical hallucination?

No two people dream the same dream. No two drug addicts or alcoholics suffer identical hallucinations (as far as I know). We are all individuals from the moment we are born to the moment we 'die' – so why should we suddenly, on the point of death, succumb to a mass delusion?

The arguments are too academic for me. Instead, I decided to carry out my own little survey. In my last book, *Voices of Love*, I asked readers who had gone through an out-of-body experience, to write and tell me about it. Here are extracts from some of the letters. Read them and make up your own mind.

Dear Doris,

In *Voices of Love* you say you would like to hear from people who have experienced a return from the dead. I had this happen to me when I was about ten (I am sixty-five now). I did not mention it to anyone until about twenty years ago and was met with scorn so I've not mentioned it since but now I'm relieved to know it was for real.

When I was ten I got rheumatic fever and was confined to bed not long before Christmas. How I passed the time I really don't know. The following summer was hot and my bedroom window was wide open day and night.

One morning as I lay in bed listening to the voices of my friends playing in our back gardens I wished I could be out there with them and tears of self-pity came into my eyes. It was the dustman's day to collect and the noise of banging bins and their cheerful shouts and laughter came nearer until they were right outside and then gradually the noise faded as they went on up the street.

The sounds of children at play also faded and finally I could hear music and choirs singing, no words, just a swelling and fading of sound. I

131

thought it was Mum's radio, or wireless as we called it then, but I quickly remembered it was not powerful enough to reach upstairs to my bedroom.

The music faded but the choir grew stronger and my bedroom seemed to have a bright, white mist in it except for the area immediately around me.

The mist gradually passed to leave a tube of light from me to somewhere in the far, unseen distance, light that grew brighter as the choir grew louder. I had the feeling of floating through the tube which was lovely. I wanted it to go on for ever. I felt warm and free of pain and quite indescribably happy, a happiness I've never experienced since. It surrounded me like a cocoon of embracing arms.

Suddenly the shouting returned, the light began to fade, I felt heavy and the pain was returning. There was a thump and feeling very surprised I opened my eyes to see our family doctor leaning over me slapping my face and shouting, 'Arthur! Come back! Come back!' My mother was rubbing my feet and legs and sobbing loudly, tears pouring down her face.

The pain and weight of the sheet which was all that covered me was so great I heard myself scream, then I fainted. When I came round the efforts of doctor and mother were still going on and I fainted again. Eventually I came round and the doctor was saying, 'It was a close thing but he'll be all right now'.

I only remember a feeling of bitter disappointment which lasted for days and days.

It was winter again before I was allowed to sit up, then weeks later I was allowed to put my legs to the floor. Obviously I made a complete recovery in the end but that was my experience of dying.

Mr A.H.
Somerset

Dear Doris,

I've just finished reading your latest book and see you want to hear from readers with 'death' experiences.

Having had five operations I know you do not dream under anaesthetic. In May 1962 I was in hospital having a kidney removed and had been returned to my room.

Suddenly I was aware of my bed being pushed forward and I went along a dark tunnel and entered a vast cavern of light, warmth and peace.

My father, who had died four months previously from cancer, was sitting on the right-hand side of a presence who I knew was God.

This presence was again a vast area of light and I tried to look behind the light but knew I wouldn't be able to. My father, looking well, relaxed and much restored, glanced towards the presence, looked back at me and smiled, but shook his head.

I was withdrawn from the scene. No word was spoken but we understood, and I was in no pain there.

I thought my father had come through to me

to let me know there was life after death. Although I thought there might be, I don't think he did!

I was awakened by a terrible scream and remember thinking, 'My God, someone is going through it here.'

There were four people, nurses and doctors, round my bed and one was shouting, 'Come on, breathe!'

I had been taught to deep breathe before the operation and I did my best. Then I felt the pain and I realized it was me who had screamed, then I fell unconscious again.

I thought they had jolted me bringing me back from the theatre and putting me in my own bed and had woken me – but the pain and the scream were in the wrong order, if you follow me.

It wasn't until years afterwards I was reading a book about life after death and read of people either leaving the body or going through a dark tunnel that I realised in a flash that I had probably 'died' for a moment and they were fighting to bring me back.

There is absolutely nothing to be feared of, it was a most beautiful experience and I feel privileged to have been there.

Mrs M.N.
Essex

134

Dear Doris,

I have just finished reading your fifth book (hope you write many more). You say you would like to hear of experiences of 'dying'.

My husband passed over in 1981 but about three years before then he had pneumonia and at his crisis point he 'died'.

I was sitting by the bed holding his hand. The room was quite dim (it was evening). There was just a small bedside lamp on for me to watch him. He suddenly put his hand up to his eyes as you do in bright sunlight. He said, 'Isn't the light bright, it's wonderful.' Then he said, 'There's my Gran and Ron amidst the flowers. I wonder where all the flowers are from, they're so beautiful.'

A little frightened, I shook him slightly and squeezed his hand. He opened his eyes then and was surprised to see me there. From then he began to improve until he was as well as he could be as he had a heart problem.

When he was well he talked to me about his experience. He said it was wonderful and the light was so bright and warm, yet nothing like sunlight. He saw his Gran (who died when he was a young boy) and Ron, his friend (killed in the Second World War), standing on the opposite bank of a river. All he had to do was cross the water after coming down a rather dark tunnel. His Gran however put up her hand and said, 'Not yet, son, later.' He thought he must have opened his eyes then.

He often said to me after, 'Don't ever be afraid of dying, it is a wonderful experience and so warm and comfortable, nothing to be afraid of. You know, if I go first I shall be waiting for you when your time comes as my Gran was waiting for me.'

Mrs W.A.
Staffordshire

Dear Doris,

The main reason I'm writing to you is because you say that you would be interested to hear from anyone else who had 'died'. This happened to me, also whilst under a general anaesthetic, and it was a most revealing experience which I am only too pleased to tell you about.

At first everything was dark and there was no noise and I thought, this is it, I must be dying. Then suddenly there was a bright light which seemed to be taking me forward and I thought, why is it that I can still think? Will something switch off my brain like a light being switched off?

The light became brighter then seemed to rise like a curtain and there before me was what seemed a never-ending, green, open space. This was still and quiet, just complete stillness, and suddenly I realized I was completely alone and had lost all contact with the human race. I was alone and isolated yet not at all afraid.

This journey I had to make entirely alone, as I did when being born came to my mind, and then I thought what a shock it would be to my family who would not be expecting me to leave. It was as if I had just walked out on them without saying goodbye.

The thought of having upset them made me sad and there was no way I could apologize to them, but soon my thoughts ran on as to what happens next. There was no one in sight and still not a sound so I did not know what to do and just stood there looking around thinking, it's best to wait.

Suddenly the light came back and blinded the view, it became brighter and brighter then suddenly vanished and I was in darkness again. I couldn't see but a voice called me, then again. I wondered if I could put a hand out which was possible, and I realized I could hear and the voice was right beside me now. After a while the blackness lifted and I could see who it was and the person was saying, 'You are all right, it's over now.'

A few days later I plucked up courage to ask if by any chance I had nearly died in the operation. They said no ...

But when it is time for me to go, I shall go willingly as I know there is nothing to fear, in fact it is a journey to look forward to when the time is right and I feel honoured to have had this experience.

Mrs E.H.
North Cornwall

Dear Doris,

In May 1963 I gave birth to twins, a boy and a girl. The boy was stillborn, the girl was born alive and well.

I had a very bad labour. I had to have forceps and I was very torn inside and I lost quite a lot of blood. I was so ill I couldn't be moved for quite a while.

After my baby boy was born I just screamed when they told me he was dead and then suddenly I felt so happy and safe I was smiling. I went down a very long, darkish path and I went through a gate at the bottom of the path into a garden full of beautiful flowers and trees.

There was lovely green grass everywhere and as I turned I saw seven mountains with a stream running below the first one. It was the greatest feeling I've ever experienced. I knew that if I went over the stream I would not be coming back.

All of a sudden I was aware of someone tapping my face and I was back giving birth to my beautiful daughter.

Whilst I was recovering in the operating theatre there was someone watching over me. He was standing in a corner all dressed in black and I knew that while he stood there I was safe. When they decided to move me he disappeared.

Mrs V.F.
Leicester

My last letter, from Mrs J.W. of Hertfordshire, tells of the time she had a wisdom tooth out under gas, twenty-five years ago. At first she had a very unpleasant dream, something that's happened to me too under gas, although my dream was quite different from Mrs W.'s, but then suddenly the nightmare evaporated and:

'... there I was in the spirit world pleading not to return. The spirits filling me with a warmth and love I'll never forget, telling me I had to return. I argued, as was my wont, wanting my own way until finally I was told it was God's will.

I turned and there was this vast light and a feeling of power and might and strength against which you did NOT argue. I went to a kind of opening flanked by four spirits (two either side). I asked that I might be gone for not too long and would someone be with me.

I was assured I'd be looked after and the feeling of love and caring from those spirits was something I'd never known. I wanted to stay.

The next thing I knew I was with my spirits in the top corner of the dentist's room looking down on myself, still enjoying the peace and love of another world. Then I heard my mother calling my name, three dentists departing from the room and the awakening from the depths of a very deep sleep ...

Mrs J.W.
Hertfordshire

I have even received a poem on the subject from Mrs Angela Ray of Buckinghamshire. Mrs Ray writes with such authority that I feel sure she too has shared this extraordinary experience.

The Land of Eternity

What is 'Goodbye'? just a word that makes us
    cry,
When a soul like a ship, pulls from shore,
In a place where I've been just last night in a
    dream,
They don't use that word anymore.
Shimmering flowers, every hue, radiant faces I
    knew
Each saying, 'Don't cry for me,
For I'm waiting for you in this world of Summers
    blue,
The Land of Eternity.'

When I asked, 'Can I stay?' they led me away
Saying, 'He says it's not yet your time,
There are songs you must sing, seeds to plant in
    the Spring
And words to be made into rhyme.'
Wide awake in my room, where they'd left sweet
    perfume,
Life's purpose seemed clearer to me
Than it would have been, had I never seen
The Land of Eternity.

Well, there you are. Fact or hallucination? It's up to you to decide.

As for me, I am quite certain in my mind that these writers have experienced the journey to the very edge of the spirit world.

This is a very difficult thing for sceptics to believe, I know, because if these people are recounting true experiences and not hallucinations, then there must be life after death. But if you admit there is life after death, then you must also admit that there must be some truth in what we mediums say and do.

Yes, it's a real problem for the sceptics, and the debate continues.

Chapter Ten

'More tea, Mrs Stokes?'

The steward, immaculately dressed in a white jacket trimmed with gold braid, leaned forward and placed a large silver teapot on the snowy cloth.

It stood there solid and elegant, its highly-polished surface reflecting the chunky silver cutlery, the slender vase of fresh flowers, the cut-crystal glassware and the pretty little table lamp.

Now that's what I call a properly laid table, I said happily to myself. I leaned back in the winged armchair and gazed around again, determined to etch every detail indelibly on my memory: pale carpet that squashed gently under foot, glittering brassware, and walls panelled in teak, mahogany and rosewood inlaid with marquetry that glowed softly in the lamplight. Outside the window, the Kent countryside rushed by.

'We've done some things in our time,' I said to John, 'but this takes some beating.'

We were spending the afternoon on the Orient Express – the unusual setting for the launch party of my last book, *Voices of Love* – and I must say it was one of the most exciting afternoons of my life.

What a magnificent train the Orient Express is. I'd heard so much about it beforehand that I feared the reality might be a little disappointing. How wrong I was. We set off on a dreary November day and from the moment we arrived at Victoria Station and saw the midnight-blue and gold train standing there like a splendid ghost from another age, it was like stepping into a dream.

The staff, all dressed in smart twenties-style uniforms, treated us like royalty. The carriages were like exquisite drawing-rooms and even the loos were splendid affairs of mahogany with solid brass fittings and lavish mosaic floors.

All afternoon I felt like a film star! It was wonderful. What's more, the party was great fun too. Celebrities such as Pete Murray and Rusty Lee mingled with publishing people and journalists, and we all sat down to a 'High Tea' of turkey and ham and salad, scones, jam and cream and a selection of delicious cakes.

I'm sure it would have been wildly fattening were it not for the fact that I could hardly eat a thing since the cutlery was so heavy for my stroke-weakened right hand that I kept dropping it. In the end I gave it up as a bad job, but it didn't matter a bit. There were so many people to talk to I scarcely had time to finish so much as a cup of tea.

The Orient Express is a legend, of course, and I was very interested to learn a little of its history. Apparently it was conceived by two men, Georges Nagelmackers and George Mortimer Pullman, and it made its first journey in October 1883.

News of the train's luxury and elegance rapidly spread and in those days before air travel, the Orient Express, which ran from Paris to Constantinople (Istanbul as it is now known) quickly established itself as the only route for the discerning who wished to travel between East and West.

Kings, maharajahs, generals and millionaires regularly used the service and the things they got up to en route make ordinary journeys by British Rail seem very dull. One maharajah was so pleased when the chef agreed to stop the train to take on board four sheep carcasses for the maharajah's curry that he gave the man a handful of pearls, rubies and emeralds as a token of appreciation.

On another occasion King Ferdinand I of Bulgaria, who as a small boy had clearly cherished a dream of becoming an engine driver, insisted on taking a turn in the driver's seat when the train passed through Bulgaria, on the grounds that it was his country and he could do as he liked. He made such a hash of it that the brakes were damaged and the train was delayed for four hours.

Then there was the famous dancer Isadora Duncan, who mesmerized the staff by wandering the corridors to the shower dressed only in a veil – 'the size of a handkerchief' according to one eyewitness.

And we mustn't forget the spies. Unable to leap on a jet in the modern manner, famous spies like Mata Hari and Sidney Reilley set off on their missions in a much more civilized style, aboard the Orient Express.

Yes, the history is really fascinating and if you'd like to know more about it, it's worth reading *Orient Express* by E.H. Cookridge.

With all those strong and often ultimately tragic personalities associated with the train, I wondered if any of them had lingered to the present day. Would the train be haunted? But as it turned out there was much too much bustle going on for me to tune in and no lost soul drew itself to my attention. Yet there was something left over from the old days. A powerful

144

atmosphere still clung to the train, too strong to be explained merely by the beautifully refurbished carriages and the period uniforms of the staff. An indefinable air of glamour and of old-world elegance hung over the place like an echo …

The launch party raced by. It quickly grew too dark to see the countryside outside the windows but nobody minded. And nobody minded where we went. As it happened, the train chugged smoothly down to Dover, stopped a while in the station and then chugged back again, but we hardly noticed. Everyone was touched by the special magic of the Orient Express and when we finally pulled into Victoria Station at the end of our trip, we were very reluctant to leave the train.

'I shall never, never forget it,' I said dreamily to John in the car on the way home.

'Neither shall I, love. Neither shall I,' he agreed.

Often, after a really wonderful outing like that, day-to-day life can be something of an anticlimax, but on this occasion I was lucky. Just a few days later there was another special event. I did a demonstration at the Barbican on Remembrance Day. Now I visit a few theatres for demonstrations and I'm happy to say that I've never once had a miserable time (I'm nervously touching wood here). The audiences are always marvellous and the atmosphere fills with love. But that night at the Barbican really was something special.

Ever since a sell-out visit last year, I'd been promising to return to the Barbican and when Laurie was organizing my schedule he realized that November was the likeliest month.

'What d'you think about November, Doris?' he

asked.

'Suits me,' I said. Then I had a thought. 'I know, let's make it Remembrance Day. After all, the demonstrations are all about remembering loved ones who've passed on.'

'Well now. Let me see,' said Laurie, getting out his diary, 'I'm not sure what date Remembrance Sunday is this year.'

'No, no, not Remembrance Sunday,' I said. 'I mean the real Remembrance day, November 11th.'

When I was a child, everything came to a halt on the eleventh hour of the eleventh day of the eleventh month; trains, buses, people walking down the streets, we all stopped for a minute's silence to remember those who had given their lives in the war. Maybe I'm old-fashioned but I don't like the way they've tinkered around with Remembrance Day in recent years, moving the ceremony to the nearest Sunday. To my mind, it's just not the same if it's not the eleventh day of the eleventh month.

Anyway, Laurie thought it was a marvellous idea and we decided to add a few special touches to the normal demonstration, in honour of the occasion.

We decorated the stage with poppies and white chrysanthemums and then, when everyone was seated, the lights were turned down low. A single spotlight illuminated the stage and into it marched a lone bugler from the Royal Artillery in full dress uniform of navy blue trimmed with red and gleaming with brass buttons.

The chattering died away as he lifted the bugle to his lips and you could have heard a pin drop as the poignant notes of the 'Last Post' reverberated around the hall.

146

It was a moving start to the evening. There was a short silence, the bugler marched smartly off, then the mood changed as my 'signature tune', 'One Day At A Time', came belting out and I walked onto the stage in my pink 'rent-a-tent', as Terry cheekily calls it.

As I was getting ready earlier that afternoon I'd tuned in to see if I could pick up something to start me off. At first nothing happened but after a while I heard the faint words '107 Andrews House' and the name 'Dolan'. Then the phone rang and somehow from then on the house was so chaotic I didn't get the chance to concentrate again.

'I normally try to tune in before the evening starts,' I explained to the audience, 'but today, what with one thing and another, I'm afraid I didn't get much time. All I picked up was part of an address I think, 107 Andrews House – or it could have been Andrews Place – and the name Dolan. Can anybody place either of them?'

My first message is always greeted by a sort of stunned silence. To most of the audience it means nothing, of course, and the person it's intended for is usually so amazed to find herself or himself singled out, that they are rendered momentarily speechless.

Undaunted, I waited patiently and after a minute or two a fair-haired woman in a blue jacket picked her way carefully down to the microphone.

'My name is Dolan,' she said, with a rather bemused expression on her face, 'and my brother lives in Andrews House.'

As she spoke a woman's voice came in clear from the other side. 'Tell her to remember me to Lillian and to John,' she instructed me.

'I've got the names Lillian and John …' I began.

'Yes. Lillian lives at 107 and John's my son.'

But the lady in my ear was rushing on. She was giving me some sort of number with a seven in it.

'Hang on a minute, lovey,' I begged her. 'You see, she's talking about John and she's giving me a number. Part of an address, I think. Seventeen, seventy … it's not just seven is it?'

There was an invisible sigh of exasperation.

'It's not an address, it's a birthday,' I was told.

'Sorry, it's a birthday,' I relayed obediently.

The woman at the microphone nodded. 'That's right, John's birthday is on the 7th.'

I don't think I ever did work out whether I was talking to her mother or her grandmother but it didn't seem to matter. The lady was too busy getting in as many family details as she could to waste time on enlightening me. She mentioned her daughter-in-law, Jan, and her granddaughter, Joanne, and good old Uncle Charlie.

'I was very lucky,' she added. 'I went over very quickly. I just went to sleep and woke up over here.'

I thought she meant by this that she'd had a stroke, but no. Apparently she had suffered a sudden heart attack after breakfast one morning and was whisked straight over. That's the way to go.

In the background I could hear other voices queuing up for a chance to speak, but the lady stayed firmly on the vibration.

'Yes, all right, I won't be a minute,' she told them. 'There's just one thing I must say,' she turned back to me. 'I'm sad because X is feeling guilty. There'd been an argument you see and we hadn't made it up. She's been feeling guilty ever since. Will you tell her I'm sorry. It was so stupid. What a waste of good time.

Please send her my love and ask her to forgive me.'

I passed this on and the woman at the microphone nodded.

'Do you know what I'm talking about?' I asked her.

'Yes, I do,' she said. 'She'll be very pleased. She has been feeling guilty.'

This message had obviously been crucial to my spirit visitor and once she'd got it across, she was willing to melt into the background and let other voices take over. There were dozens of them, all eager to talk to their families and friends. So eager, in fact, that for the next few minutes I had a right old mix-up.

I ended up with two young girls at the microphone, one dark haired and bubbly, the other blonde and tearful. The dark-haired girl had a mother in spirit who was most anxious to talk to her, while the blonde had a father on the spirit side who felt the same.

They both decided to talk at the same time and the messages came out in a tangle. In the end the conversation went backwards and forwards between the two of them like a tennis ball at Wimbledon.

Basically, it seemed that the father of the blonde ('Call her Nelly and make her laugh,' he said. 'Her name's Ellen.') wanted her to know that although he, too, had died unexpectedly young of a heart attack, he was now well and happy on the other side with Ellen's grandparents, Frank and Ellen. 'We're looking after him, girl,' Frank told his granddaughter. 'Dry your eyes.'

The brunette's mother was keen for her daughter to understand that she was still around and knew exactly what was going on.

'She's moving, you know,' she told me, settling

down for a bit of a gossip, 'and they're knocking out the fireplace.'

'Well, we're hoping to when we've moved in,' agreed the daughter.

'And she's getting a new washing machine.'

'I'm not sure about that,' said the girl.

'Yes she is, she needs one,' insisted her mother. 'Her old one was second hand. It only cost £70. It did her a good turn but it's past it now. She needs a new one.'

'Well, your mum says you're to have one,' I told her.

She went on to send her love to her other daughter, Cheryl, a hairdresser, who'd been a bit unhappy lately.

And so it went on. Many of the contacts had a few light-hearted words to cheer their relatives but some could not hide the sadness surrounding their passing.

One pale, drawn lady in sombre clothes was overcome to be reunited with mother hen. She was only thirteen years old when her beloved mum passed over.

'It shouldn't have happened. Something went wrong,' complained the mother.

Apparently, she had gone into hospital for an operation which appeared to be successful, and then a few days later she suddenly became ill and died. Nevertheless, she had stayed close to her daughter all these years, she'd watched over her little grandson, Robert, when he was born and now she brought back with her a beautiful two-year-old girl with auburn hair to show me.

'Did you lose a child?' I asked the lady at the microphone.

'Yes, I had a miscarriage.'

150

'Well, it was a little girl and she's got auburn hair,' I told her.

The woman gasped. 'My little boy's got auburn hair,' she said.

'So has your little girl,' I explained.

'We've called her Claire,' put in the proud grandmother in the spirit world. 'And there's no need to worry because I'm bringing her up now.'

There were quite a few young people who'd passed at a tragically young age. The most horrifying of all came right at the end. A boy whom I at first took to have been murdered moved in close.

'Ireland,' I heard him say. Then I felt a stabbing sensation. Immediately I had the sense of a lung being punctured and filling with blood, followed by a choking, drowning feeling. He had drowned in his own blood.

Putting the two together, I jumped to the conclusion that the lad had been murdered in Ireland.

The elderly, white-haired lady who'd claimed him, hitched her blue cardigan more comfortably round her shoulders and shook her head.

'No, he wasn't murdered,' she said. 'He did it himself. He'd just come back from Ireland.'

'He did it himself!' I was so shocked that for a moment I was speechless. Of all the ways to take yourself over, what a dreadful thing to choose. The boy was obviously very, very sick at the time.

'They tried to save me,' he said regretfully, 'but by the time they got me to hospital it was too late.'

It was a downbeat note to end the evening but fortunately there was a happy surprise in store for the audience before they went home. Sally Whittaker from *Coronation Street* had come along to give out the flowers, a little ceremony which has become a permanent fixture of these evenings. She moved tirelessly up and down the stage, distributing bouquets to people who had received messages, and shaking hands.

I hope the recipients think of these flowers as coming not from Laurie and me, but from their loved ones on the other side who would jump at the chance to give them such a gift if only they could.

Sadly, I couldn't hang around chatting for long after the show because I had to dash home for a live phone-in from Australia, but even though it ended rather abruptly as far as I was concerned, the evening stands out in my mind as a special one. It would be nice to do a regular November 11th appearance every year. I know we remember our family and friends in spirit every day, but Remembrance Day seems particularly appropriate.

It wasn't just me being sentimental. I think some members of the audience sensed the special quality that was in the air that night because, afterwards, a lady called Pam Lyons sent me a beautiful poem she'd written immediately after the show. Apparently she couldn't go to bed until she'd written down the words that came into her head, inspired by the events of the evening. The poem goes like this:

> Step across tomorrow, past all your yesterdays,
> Feel their love surround you in soft caressing waves.
>
> Know that all who've gone before
> Walk with you hand in hand

For they are ever watchful, in a place called
Morningland.
And sorrow cannot hurt you, and grief it does
not last.
But Love endures forever,
Though eternity should pass.

I travel to a lot of theatres these days and inevitably
one occasion tends to blur into another in my mind.
Every evening is a marvellous experience because the
people are so warm and make me feel so welcome.
Yet, just as in any other job, I find that some nights
things work better than others.

It's a bit like driving a car. Some days you get in the
car and although you feel perfectly well, you can't
seem to do a thing right. Your co-ordination's a little
bit out; you stall at the traffic lights, make a hash of
reversing, crash the gears like a learner and fail to
overtake when it is perfectly safe. Other days you
jump in the car, pull easily away and everything falls
fluidly into place; you sail along, smooth as a dream,
the controls just extensions of your own body.

It's just the same being a medium. There are nights
when I have to struggle for every contact and sort
through a jumble of messages as confusing as tangled
knitting; and there are other nights when one message flows easily into the next, clear, precise and
accurate. I don't know why it should be like that but
it is, and obviously it's the extremes that tend to stand
out in the memory.

I had a wonderful evening recently when I went to
Lewisham. I tend to appear at Lewisham Theatre more
frequently than anywhere else because it's my 'local'! I

don't have to spend hours on the motorway to get there and I don't have to book into a hotel for the night or worry about packing cases for the visit. It might sound dull but, quite honestly, at my age these benefits are becoming increasingly attractive.

Anyway, once again I was standing on the familiar stage at Lewisham and suddenly, almost as if my brain clicked into overdrive, the voices came flying through.

To open the evening I got my first contact to pass with AIDS. I suspect I'm going to get a lot more of these in the coming months but this was my first confirmed case. The poor lad, Simon I think his name was, came back full of love for his boyfriend who had nursed him devotedly through the terrible ordeal.

Simon mentioned a great many family members and friends but most of all he wanted to reassure his lover that he was now fit and well and happy. They were obviously very close indeed and he promised that he wouldn't move on in the spirit world. He would wait faithfully for his friend and then they would progress together.

Alarmed as I am about the spread of AIDS, I feel nothing but pity for the sufferers. I can't understand how people can be cruel to these poor victims who often go through agonies before they pass, and I made a special point to ask the red-eyed boy at the microphone to make sure he stayed behind to collect some flowers from his friend.

After a long chat, Simon stood back to allow other voices to come through and immediately a little girl piped up:

'I'm Michelle and it's my anniversary this month and my mum and dad are here.'

When spirit people talk about anniversaries, they

mean the anniversary of their passing which to them is like a birthday.

'Does anyone know a Michelle who's got an anniversary coming up?' I asked.

Down in the audience I saw a head bob up and a woman hurried down to the microphone.

'Do you know a Michelle, love, and is there an anniversary?' I asked.

'Yes, she's my daughter and the anniversary is today.'

'Tell her that Peter's here with me,' said Michelle. 'Oh, and there's my dad.'

I glanced up as a man started threading his way along the row of seats to join his wife at the microphone.

'Peter's with her,' I continued to the woman.

'That's my father,' she said.

By this time the man had reached his wife and I was just about to go on when something struck me about the faces of the couple. They looked oddly familiar.

'I've spoken to you before, haven't I?' I asked.

'Well, yes you have, Doris,' they admitted. 'We came to see you last year.'

I had no idea they were going to be present that night and I had no idea of the date of Michelle's passing. In fact, I could remember nothing of the sitting apart from the fact that the little girl had passed tragically in some sort of accident. When you talk to as many people as I do, you can't possibly remember the names of their families and friends and all the intimate details they tell you. Nevertheless, it was only fair that I told the audience what had happened.

155

'Well, Michelle,' I said when I'd finished explaining, 'you'd better tell me about things that have happened recently or I'll be accused of just remembering what you told me last time.'

'Mummy and Daddy have bought a new car,' she volunteered.

'Yes, we've bought another taxi,' her father agreed.

There was something muffled about a move.

'Her friends have just moved to a new house,' said her mother.

'And Daddy bought Mummy a new watch.'

'Yes, he did.'

'Then there's Billy.'

'That's my little boy's little friend.'

'I didn't know him before but I do now,' said Michelle. 'He's always into things and my brother gets the blame.'

Very faintly beside Michelle I heard another voice. It was so indistinct I couldn't tell if it was male or female, but the person just managed to get over that they'd passed with lung cancer.

'Oh yes,' said Michelle's mother. 'My aunt died two weeks ago.'

'Don't forget Joyce,' said Michelle.

'No, Josie,' said her mother. 'That's her friend round the corner.'

'Sorry, Michelle, my mistake, I thought you said Joyce,' I apologized.

'Josie's got a new dog now,' said Michelle. 'Well you did want to know what's been happening lately. And Mummy's had her ears pierced.'

'Yes, I have,' gasped her mother, her hands going involuntarily to her ears.

Michelle started giggling, so loudly in fact that I

couldn't make out her next words. It was something about painting and George. 'George did it,' was all I could hear clearly.

Her mother laughed. 'Yes, I know what that's about. George is her uncle and he is painting the house for the friends who've recently moved.'

'Then there's Patrick.'

'That's a friend at work,' said Michelle's mother.

'Mummy works in a ...' It went a bit muzzy. 'Hospital,' I thought she said. But just as I was about to say it I caught a glimpse of a pretty child with the most beautiful copper hair. She put her hand on her hip in exasperation and wagged her finger at me.

'You're not listening, Doris,' she complained. 'I didn't say hospital, I said school. Mummy works in a school.'

'Yes, I do,' said her mother, 'I clean a school.'

And so it went on. Michelle was able to communicate well because she'd done it before and that helps. It's almost as difficult for them as it is for me. We have to work very hard at both ends to get the message across. But although it's easier when the spirit person has communicated before, it's not essential. If the link of love is strong enough, if the need is urgent enough, the spirit people get through.

And get through they did that night. Very little went wrong.

Towards the end there came another daughter tragically killed. Eighteen-year-old Susan had passed in a road accident. Her face hadn't been marked but she was in a coma. Apparently for forty-eight hours the doctors thought there might be some hope, but then she sank deeper and they realized there was nothing they could do.

As we talked, Susan showed me a picture. I was looking at a gravestone in the shape of an open book, and written on it I could see the words 'Safe in the arms ...'

'Yes, that's right,' said Susan's mother when I described what I had seen. 'That's her grave.'

'It's very nice,' said Susan, 'and I sit with Mum when she goes to visit it, but then I go home with her again. She doesn't have to go to the grave to talk to me, I'm with her a lot.

'You know what's really been bothering her? Just before it happened I was a bridesmaid and now she keeps thinking of that song: 'Always the Bridesmaid, Never the Blushing Bride' – and it upsets her that I wasn't ever a bride. But it doesn't matter at all. I'm happy here.'

Like most spirit people, Susan had looked in on her own funeral and she was particularly proud of the cross of white flowers given to her by her family and the heart of flowers from her boyfriend.

'But, you know, all you need to do is give her a fresh flower by her photograph,' I explained to her mother. 'She'll be happy to see that when she visits you at home.'

And of course to start her off, I gave her some flowers from the stage.

The voices went on and on. While I stood there under the lights I felt as if I could go on all night. I was so full of energy and strength I thought I could do anything. But what a shock I was in for when the evening finished. Nothing's for nothing, as they say, and I had to pay for all that energy I'd used. Suddenly I was so exhausted I had to be helped back to the dressing-room and I sat there for ages like a wrung-out dishcloth, too tired even to talk.

I was weary for days afterwards, but I must say it was worth it. Long after the memory of exhaustion has faded, I shall remember that wonderful evening at Lewisham.

Chapter Eleven

John Morley, my accountant, shook his head.

'Really, Doris. Your phone bill. It's astronomical.'
He leafed disbelievingly through the blue and white
sheets. 'You'll have to do something about this you
know. You'll have to cut down.'

I stared sadly at the little heap of bills. 'I know. It's
awful, isn't it,' I said, 'but there's nothing I can do.
Often I just have to phone people urgently.'

How could I explain to my accountant the sort of
letters I get which just cry out for an immediate
answer? Only a few days before, for instance, the post
brought me a desperate appeal from a lady who had
murdered her baby when it was only five months old.
She had been in purgatory ever since.

Even before I finished reading the tragic lines, I
sensed Ramanov with me, urging me to pick up the
phone and dial the number printed at the top of the
page.

The poor woman was in a terrible state. When I
tuned in, her relatives in the spirit world told me that
she had been suffering from post-natal depression and
wasn't to be blamed. In fact, even in this world she
wasn't blamed and people had tried to help her.

'I know,' sobbed the woman, 'that's what made me
feel so guilty. Instead of being punished, people tried

to help me. I should have been punished for what I did.'

She had been carrying this dreadful burden around for years. It took quite a while for the spirit world to convince her that she truly wasn't to blame because she was sick, and that even her child didn't blame her.

Obviously, as this emotional call went on the little meter was ticking away, but what can you do? These things are important.

Then there was the case of a poor girl who was highly distressed because a medium had told her that her beloved husband was in 'limbo'. Once again I felt compelled to phone her and it was a good thing I did. She, too, was in a bad way.

She wasn't very old and apparently on her birthday her husband had taken her out for a treat. They had a nice evening, came home, and the husband sat down on the sofa while his wife put the kettle on. The next thing the girl knew, he'd keeled over, collapsed and 'died'.

Naturally she was distraught. There had been no hint of any ill-health in her husband and he was still a young man. What's more, the couple had two small children and they had looked forward to many happy years ahead with their family.

Shocked and unhappy, the young widow consulted a medium, hoping for comfort. What she got was an increase of agony.

The medium told her that because her husband had passed so suddenly and unexpectedly, he was in 'limbo' and for this reason the medium was unable to contact him. The poor girl came away almost out of her mind with worry, imagining that her husband was floating around aimlessly somewhere, belonging neither to this world nor the next.

I felt desperately sorry for her and furious with the medium. Honestly, I don't know where some people who call themselves mediums get their ideas, I really don't. This theory about limbo goes against everything I've been taught by the spirit world.

Anyway, I telephoned the girl, tuned in and her husband came to us straight away. He wasn't in limbo, he was safely in the spirit world and his only worry was the distress his wife was suffering.

He gave me his name, which was Ashley, if I remember correctly. He talked of the way he passed, of his family and of someone called John who had been a godsend to his wife and helped her sort out the complicated business that always accompanies a bereavement. Just as we were winding up, he said, 'There will be some flowers.'

But I thought no, that's your mind butting in, Doris. Earlier I'd been thinking what a shame it was that there were no fresh flowers in the house. I'm letting my own thoughts intrude, I said to myself sternly. If my concentration was going it was just as well the little sitting was over. So I said goodbye to the girl who was now more cheerful and I didn't mention the last bit about the flowers.

As usual, though, I shouldn't have doubted. The following Monday morning a beautiful bouquet arrived with a little card from the young widow thanking me for all the comfort and strength I had given her. That last message had been from Ashley after all.

Not long after this I had another query about limbo. How it seems to worry people. A lady wrote to say that her husband had passed over and left instructions that he should be cremated. She had respected his wishes and had the body cremated but afterwards she was very upset by a remark his sister had made. Apparently the sister was of the opinion that her brother was now in limbo because his soul had been burnt.

I've never heard such nonsense. You can't burn a soul. It's simply not possible. All you burn when a body is cremated is the soul's old overcoat for which it no longer has a use.

'I don't know, John,' I said, when I'd finished reading the letter, 'this limbo bit again. We're going to be cremated, aren't we? Our old clothes won't be any use to us when we're away. When medical science has finished with my body I don't care what happens to it.'

For some reason this episode set me thinking about funerals and the things people have written on their loved ones' tombstones as epitaphs, and as these thoughts passed through my head, I suddenly heard a spirit voice recite the perfect epitaph:

'Your work on earth is finished, Your life in spirit has begun, When you stand before the master, We know he'll say well done.'

What a beautiful verse, I thought, and how wonderful if it could be true. It's certainly something we should all aim for.

So you see, when I sat there listening to the accountant taking me to task over my phone bill it was impossible for me to promise to mend my ways.

'I know it costs a fortune,' I explained, 'but there's really nothing I can do about it. The phone calls are part of my work and I have to make them.'

But you don't have to be a medium in order to try to live your life well and make your spirit people proud of you. We can all do our bit in our own little way and it's amazing how one kind act can spread and spread.

My father always used to quote the old song: 'If you have a kindness shown you, pass it on. It's not meant for you alone ... pass it on.'

And it's so true. It's quite extraordinary what happens when you start passing kindness on. Recently we had this demonstrated in the most practical way.

Tom Johanson from the SAGB (The Spiritualist Association of Great Britain) phoned Laurie to ask if there was any way in which we could help with the renovation work necessary at the Association's head office in Belgrave Square. The building is very old, it requires a lot of looking after and money is tight.

Well, first of all, Laurie and I suggested that we pay for a room to be decorated, providing materials and labour. Tom thanked us but explained that they had quite a number of volunteers going in at weekends to help with the decorating. No, what they were in desperate need of, he explained, was some new chairs for the restaurant.

Naturally, Laurie and I agreed to buy the chairs, and somehow we ended up buying the tables to go with them as well.

When Tom wrote to thank us he explained that after receiving our gift, Fulham Church had got in touch with the news that they needed new tables. So Tom gave them the old tables from SAGB, together with the new tablecloths they'd bought, because the tables Laurie and I had sent didn't need cloths. What's more, he added, since then SAGB had been given another forty chairs.

Hardly had we finished reading the letter when

someone rang up from Sheerness with another plea. They had been given a building for a church and did we know anyone who'd got any chairs?

The upshot was that Terry went to SAGB, loaded the spare chairs into his van and drove them down to Sheerness where they are now installed in the new church.

That one act of kindness resulted in three churches benefiting. It just shows that good deeds aren't wasted.

Mind you, you don't often see such a clear-cut case as this. Most of the time, I know, it often feels as if there's so much wickedness in the world that good doesn't stand a chance. New horrors seem to crop up every day and the latest dreadful worry is AIDS.

Jean and I were talking about it not long ago. As I think I've explained, since my stroke all the strength seems to have gone out of my right arm and it shakes quite a bit so I've had to get someone to help with the housework. Jean is a marvel and recently she's become indispensable. She's started coming to theatres with me to help me with my zips and the unpacking and repacking of my long stage dresses. On the last journey she even ended up doing the navigating.

'Is there no end to your talents, Jean?' we teased, as she successfully guided us into the town centre despite one-way systems and all manner of fiendishly confusing traffic signs.

So brilliant is Jean in every way that we've jokingly nicknamed her 'Treasure', and it's caught on to such an extent that now at the theatres everyone calls out for 'Treasure'.

Anyway, this particular day the subject of AIDS

came up and Jean said how worried she was about it, not for herself, but for her grandchildren.

'I'm well on the way now,' said Jean, 'but what about the young people? What's going to happen to my grandchildren? The way things are going they could all be wiped out.'

I brooded on the question long after she'd gone and I got myself pretty depressed. It began to seem as if God had got fed up with us at last and this was his punishment.

The idea frightened me so much that that night when I sat down to tune in to my guide Ramanov, I had to ask him about it.

'Ramanov,' I said, 'I've been thinking about this terrible AIDS epidemic and all the suffering it's going to cause. Is God punishing us?'

'No, child,' Ramanov replied in his calm, reasonable way, 'it's not God punishing you. You are punishing yourselves. You each know your own moral responsibilities. You know your responsibilities to your families and to the world.

'If you ignore the rules then this is the sort of thing that happens. It's not God. It's a weakness in mankind. You don't have to behave the way you do, you are free to choose. But if you knowingly take the wrong path then you have to accept the consequences.'

I wasn't sure whether this comforted me or not. Once again, it seemed, innocent people were going to suffer for the mistakes of others. Life is very unfair. Thank goodness you don't get this sort of injustice in the spirit world.

I try to tune in to Ramanov every night and he always comes to talk to me. He must be a saint because sometimes I'm sure he gets fed up with me forever whingeing about something. If I was him, I'd have earache by now!

Recently, I was moaning on about a very hurtful article in a newspaper. It was my usual theme to Ramanov about working so hard and yet being so misunderstood.

'I don't know,' I went on, 'I sometimes wonder if it's worth it. All this aggravation and worry ...'

'Now look,' interrupted Ramanov in the nearest he ever came to an impatient voice, 'I didn't promise you roses all the way, did I? I didn't even promise to take the stones out of the pathway.'

'No,' I admitted reluctantly, 'you didn't.'

'Well then. These difficulties are there for you to overcome and to grow stronger in the overcoming. Anything worth having is worth fighting for. So long as you know within your heart that you are doing the right thing and you are playing fair with the spirit world and being honest – then that's all that matters. You will triumph in the end.'

Well, that was me told in no uncertain terms. I didn't dare complain again for at least a week after that!

Ramanov was certainly right when he said that anything worth having is worth fighting for. I seem to have been fighting ever since I was a medium. It was only after he'd given me his little lecture that I remembered I've always suffered various kinds of aggravation ever since I've been a medium.

Maybe it's because I'm a bit of a rebel and I've always gone my own way, but somehow I was always getting myself into trouble.

When I was a young medium living in Lancaster I used to work for the local spiritualist churches.

Occasionally though, people would ring and plead for a private sitting. Some of them came from as far afield as America or Egypt and it was very difficult to say no. I couldn't understand why I should say no. They needed help and I was able to give it. What on earth could be wrong with that?

We were very hard up in those days because John with his war wounds couldn't earn much money and his pension didn't go far, so I used to charge one pound for my sittings. These days, thank goodness, we don't have to struggle and I don't charge at all for the few sittings I'm able to do, but back then the money was a great help.

Anyway, I did my sittings but for some reason the church didn't like it. How they got to know I can't imagine, but I can guarantee that within a day or two of a sitting a letter would arrive from the secretary of the church committee:

Dear Mrs Stokes,

It's come to my notice that you have been doing private sittings. If you continue to do private sittings I'm afraid we will have to expel you from the church.

Yours etc.

It was like being back at school but as an ex-nurse I had a healthy respect for authority and these letters used to frighten me. Afterwards, I would do my best to tow the line, until the next desperate appeal landed me in trouble again.

I just couldn't understand what I was doing wrong. If I'd turned up drunk at church meetings or used foul language or had an affair with someone else's husband I could understand the committee feeling it had to take a stand, but what could be wrong with helping people?

The last straw came when a family arrived on my doorstep frantic with grief over the loss of a son. The sitting went very well and they left my house like different people. Heads held high, tears gone and a new spirit of hope in their step.

Two days later I opened the mail and there it was:

Dear Mrs Stokes,

   It has come to my notice that ...

I was furious. I was so incensed that there and then I phoned the late Richard Eldridge, then president of the National Union.

'I'm ringing to tell you that I'm sending my credential cards back,' I told him. 'And as far as I'm concerned you know what you can do with them.'

A medium is awarded her credential cards after passing a strict test. These cards permit you to work in spiritualist churches and with the public. No medium is considered qualified without her 'credentials'.

Richard, who probably scarcely knew who I was, was rather taken aback.

'Why's that, Doris?' he asked mildy.

'I'm just a little bit tired of the church committee interfering every time I try to do something to help people outside the church,' I exploded.

Richard was very good. He soothed my anger, calmed me down and then got me to explain slowly just what had been happening to upset me so.

When I'd finished, he promised to look into the matter. Sure enough, after that, the unpleasant little notes stopped. But what a shame the situation had had to reach that pitch. The energy I wasted in indignation. The energy the committee secretary wasted writing those unnecessary letters. And the years that were wasted when I could have been going forward and helping people but was held back by stupid rules and regulations.

Sadly, it still goes on today. I'm afraid we still get a few self-important people trying to push the youngsters around and coming out with a load of nonsense in the process. A few years ago, when I lived in Fulham, I used to run a teaching class for developing mediums.

I sat in a circle with the kids, we said a prayer and then we tuned in. One day, just as we were settling down, one of the boys said:

'You have to keep both feet on the floor, you know, or it doesn't work.'

At his words the years rolled back and I remembered being told the very same thing myself.

'That's what I was told, too, son,' I said. 'And it's not true. It doesn't matter. You can take your shoes off, sit on your feet or stand on your head, if you want to. It doesn't make a blind bit of difference.

'I was also told that you needed a dim light and a bowl of clear water in the room. It's a load of nonsense. You can tune in at any time, in any place, so long as you can concentrate.'

170

Perhaps I was teaching my youngsters to be rebels too, I don't know. My only thought was to make sure their heads weren't filled with a load of rubbish.

Funnily enough, even today at my age I still have problems from time to time with the spiritualist 'establishment'. I was expecting a lot of criticism earlier in the year when I agreed to appear on the Jasper Carrott show.

It was Jasper's producer who first contacted Laurie to ask if I would do it. Laurie's immediate reaction was no. He tends to be very protective of me. Jasper's show is a satirical programme, after all, and mediums are fair game for being sent up at the best of times without actually setting themselves up for it.

'It's very kind of you,' said Laurie, politely. 'But I really don't think it's Doris's cup of tea.'

The next day, however, Jasper himself phoned me at home.

'Doris, I've been following your career for years and I've got the greatest respect for you,' he said.

I listened carefully for a mocking note in his voice but I could detect nothing.

'We'd really like you to do this,' Jasper went on. 'I'll send you the script and if there's anything you don't like, you can change it.'

He was so charming I could feel myself being persuaded.

'You promise you're not going to send up spiritualism?'

He promised. And he was as good as his word. When the script arrived I saw that the scene they wanted me to take part in was an amusing sketch about British Telecom and how difficult it is to get through to directory enquiries. It takes a medium to get a reply, they implied.

No-one with a sense of humour could object. There was nothing offensive in it. The only thing I didn't like was the fact that they'd got the medium working in a darkened room. I never work in the dark. All that darkened room stuff is just part of the old superstitious mumbo jumbo. The brighter the sunshine the better it suits me.

'Yes, I'll do it,' I told them when they phoned to see what I thought of the script. 'The only thing I don't like is the darkened room bit. Everything I do is in full light so I would be very pleased if you cut that out.'

There was no fuss. They agreed immediately and I had a very enjoyable time. Jasper came to see me on set. He kissed me and asked if everything was all right, whether I wanted to change the script in any way, whether there was anything I wanted taken away or added.

'No, it's fine now, Jasper,' I assured him. 'Now they've taken out that darkened room bit, I'm happy.'

Throughout the show everyone treated me with the greatest respect and when I eventually saw the finished product on screen I still thought it was amusing. The whole thing went so well that if there's ever anything else I can do for Jasper, I'd be glad to.

The day the programme went out I waited for the criticism but, surprisingly enough, there was hardly a murmur. Perhaps the dour members of the 'establishment' don't watch Jasper Carrott. Or perhaps they have acquired a sense of humour at last.

Whatever the reason, I'll never again let them put me off doing something I believe is right. It's lonely going against the group but I'll follow Ramanov's advice from now on. If I know in my heart that what

172

I'm doing is right, if I'm being fair with the spirit world and I'm being honest – then I'll go right ahead and do it.

Incidentally, just to prove that I'm not the only one who gets encouragement from the spirit world, and that you don't have to be a medium to hear voices, I must tell you a lovely little story.

The other day I heard from an elderly lady in her eighties who was very puzzled and somewhat alarmed to hear a disembodied voice speaking to her.

As far as she knew she wasn't psychic, and she'd never in her life before had an experience like this. Nevertheless, one night just after she'd gone to bed, she distinctly heard a voice speaking to her from somewhere behind her head.

The voice was definitely outside her head but there was no one else in the flat and the people next door had gone to bed long ago. The voice was very beautiful, though she couldn't really tell whether it was male or female and she was quite certain she'd never heard it before.

'The waters of the Lord floweth over me,' it said. 'And I was made whole.'

That was all it said and then there was silence. Now the lady puzzled over those words for the rest of the night. They sounded almost like a quotation but though she scoured her *Dictionary of Quotations* very carefully she couldn't find the source. She began to wonder whether she was going mad, and that's when she asked what I thought of the matter.

Well, of course, I knew straight away that she wasn't going mad but I could understand how she felt. Hadn't I often feared that I was going round the bend in the early days when spirit people kept talking to me and my family thought I was peculiar?

'No, dear, you're as sane as can be,' I assured her. Had she been ill recently, I wondered?

It turned out that this lady had been suffering for months after an unpleasant operation. Often she got very depressed about it which wasn't at all surprising.

The answer was clear to me. The spirit world knew what she was going through and were trying to re-assure her that she wasn't alone. Despite her trials and tribulations she was gradually getting better and must not lose heart.

I thought it was a lovely story and it just proves that when we are most in need the spirit world doesn't let us down. Not everyone will hear voices of course; some might feel a loving presence, others might be mystified by peculiar happenings in the home or a chain of coincidences too unlikely to be called coincidence.

The spirit world finds many different ways to put its message across. The important thing is that we are not alone and when we need help we need only stretch out our hands and it will be there.

Just to cheer me even more, I heard, about this time, from a Roman Catholic priest who became a member of my Sod-It-Club last year.

I was in hospital when I met him and the poor man was terrified because he had cancer in the leg and he dreaded having the leg amputated. He was talking to me about it one day before his operation and I said, 'Father, why don't you join the Sod-It-Club?'

He looked a bit taken aback. 'What's that, love?' he asked.

So I told him the club's history and how Diana Dors and Pat Pheonix, among others, had all found it comforting.

'So when you go down to theatre say, "Sod it! I'm not going to lose my leg. They are not going to take my leg off,"' I finished.

The priest roared with laughter and agreed that, put like that, you couldn't really call it swearing.

Anyway, he had his operation and, after they had wheeled him back to his bed, the sister who'd been in the theatre with him popped her head round my door.

'Do you know, after his pre-med when he was floating on air, all we could hear was this mumbled voice saying, "Sod it, they're not going to take my leg off. Sod it, they're not going to take my leg off." The surgeons couldn't believe it from a priest!'

Months later the priest phoned me.

'I just wanted to tell you, lovey, that it worked,' he said. 'I've got a stiff leg now but I haven't lost it. I put it down to the Sod-It-Club!'

Chapter Twelve

Once again this year I've been inundated with poems.
What a talented lot my readers are! I do enjoy reading
them. Somehow you can sum up in a few lines of
poetry sentiments that would take pages and pages of
ordinary prose. A couple of verses on a single sheet
can make you laugh, make you cry or can give you
something to think about for the rest of the day. It's
amazing the power of poetry.

As I've explained before, I simply haven't the space
to publish all the works I'm sent. There's only room
for a tiny selection to whet the appetite and, with a
bit of luck, to inspire other budding poets to put pen
to paper.

Ann Fairman sent me this first one. It's a humorous
poem and I must say I particularly enjoy these. I come
across so much tragedy in the world that laughter is a
specially precious gift to me. Nothing is quite so bad
if you can have a laugh. Even when you're ill, laughter
makes you feel better. Frankly, without a sense of
humour I don't know what I'd do sometimes.

Our Doris

A medium known as 'Our Doris'
Made contact with Great Uncle Horace.
He said, 'Hello, dear. It's lovely up here
And today I met my brother Maurice.
He passed on in his sleep as he lay in a heap
And I greeted him on his arrival,
He said, 'Hello, Mate,' as I opened the gate,
'So this is what's known as 'survival'.

'Well isn't it nice! So warm and loving,
All pain and distress left behind.
And here's Auntie Lil and our Uncle Bill,
They've both come to meet me, how kind!'

Now I don't wish to gloat 'cos I've shed my old
    coat,
But there's nothing to fear, that's a promise,
If you want to know more then pop down to the
    store,
And buy all those books by 'Our Doris'.

                                        Ann Fairman

Ann has certainly captured the spirit of 'survival'
without preaching to anyone and I must say I can't
argue with the sentiments in the last line!

This next poem made me laugh too. Unfortunately,
it's become detached from its accompanying letter so
I don't have an author's name or a title, but it's such
fun that it seemed a shame not to share it. So, with
apologies to the author, here it is:

I dreamt of heaven the other night
And the pearly gates swung wide
An Angel with a halo bright
Ushered me inside.

And there to my astonishment
Stood folks I'd judged and labelled
As quite 'unfit', of little worth,
And spiritually disabled.

Indignant words rose to my lips
But never were set free
For every face showed stunned surprise –
Not one expected me.

You can't help smiling, can you, yet in twelve short, amusing lines the author has created a lesson for us all. I'll have to bite my tongue before I have a moan about anyone again.

Now if the inclusion of *Medium Rare* seems like sheer indulgence, please forgive me. All I can say in my own defence is that people like me have to take a lot of stick. You expect it, but it still hurts however much you try to pretend it doesn't.

Some black days it seems as if all people want to do is criticize, no matter how hard you work. On days like that you tend to think, is it worth it? Maybe I should retire and escape all this stress and heartache. Then the post arrives and out comes a poem like *Medium Rare* and suddenly everything's all right again.

Many thanks, Rene Stanton, for this uplifting poem.

Platform idol to so many folks
Is lovely, natural Doris Stokes.
Sense of humour, with serious side,
Talent spread so far and wide.
Health setbacks are overcome
Conditions that would silence some.
Doris tho' springs back with ease
Surely everyone agrees
She has no need to 'act a part'
Sincerity comes from the heart,
Long may she reign and gather strength
To live a life of greater length,
Scattering comfort on the way
Like sunshine in a sky of grey!

Rene Stanton

Well, I don't know if I can live up to all that, Rene, but I'll certainly try.

Many poems, of course, are very serious and some of them are truly inspirational. I particularly like this one by Lily Godliman. Her daughter, Kathy King, from Basildon, sent it to me with the following letter of explanation:

Dear Doris,
This poem was written by my mother, Lily Godliman, years ago. My mum died in November '85. She was only sixty-one years old. My sisters and I stayed all night at the hospital and she died

at 9 a.m. the next morning. We went back to my sister's in great shock and grief. My sister got the poem and read it to us and it was like Mum wrote it for such a time.

Mum could write lovely poems and she always wrote in cards when she sent them. She was a nurse and very caring. She would always sit with someone when they were dying and comfort them.

Her kidneys packed up and she was too ill to be moved to London for a kidney machine. We were shocked that there were none at Basildon Hospital.

We have been raising money for kidney research and are going to send it on the anniversary of Mum's death. It makes us feel better to try and help people the way Mum would and it makes life feel worth while.

I would be very happy if you used this poem in your books.

God Bless,
Kathy King

Well, I'm more than happy to use Lily's poem. I think it's beautiful.

Life is just a testing time while we are here on
    earth,
The pain and grief, the obstacles
Are all to try our worth.
It's very hard not to succumb
When things are getting tough

But you must fight and overcome
Just coping's not enough.
For living's really wonderful
The good times and the bad.
Who'd appreciate the happy days
If they'd never known the bad?
Listen to the birds at dawn
Or watch a rose unfurl
Gaze on a baby's sleeping face
Or touch a tiny curl.
So when you're feeling down and out
Your spirit is depressed,
Just look around at everything
With which you have been blessed.

Lily Godliman

Even if Kathy hadn't written to tell me of her mother's warm and loving nature, I would have known from reading these lines what a very special person she was and still is, of course, on the other side. The poem shows great spiritual understanding and it's quite clear that Lily went over so soon because she had little left to learn. She'd acquired a great deal of wisdom in her sixty-one years.

Just reading her poem does you good. I'm no angel and like everyone else I grumble now and then about my troubles. But when I read Lily's work it reminds me to count my blessings. After all, life is wonderful and we shouldn't take it for granted.

Some poets write to entertain, some to inspire, while others write of deeply personal and often tragic experiences as if the very writing of them helps ease

181

the pain. These poems are often sad, yet reading them it becomes clear that the writer, in the midst of his or her grief, has stumbled across a greater truth, a greater strength, which helps him to cope.

This poem, untitled and unsigned, is about the special grief that accompanies a stillbirth. Reading between the lines, I would say that the author must have had direct personal experience of such a tragedy, in order to write so movingly.

The mother of a stillborn child goes through a unique kind of agony and I know it well. Years ago, on a cold, bleak February day, my longed-for daughter was born 'dead'. As well as the grief it's a very lonely time for the parents because people who haven't experienced it can't understand why you mourn so for a child you've never known.

The writer of these haunting words sums up, far better than I could, the terrible sense of loss and grief for what might have been. Yet, for all that, it's a comforting poem:

God has a special place for stillborn things,
The things that never were and should have
   been:
The little songs no singer ever sings,
The beauty of a picture hung unseen,
A noble heart that loved with no return
And deeds well meant which somehow turned
   out ill,
A lovely flame that vainly tried to burn
But could not last, though all the winds were
   still,
The early flower that no one ever sees

Making its way through ground iced hard with
    sleet,
A leader to whom no man bends his knees,
The Christ-like smile that greets each fresh
    defeat;
God treats them very tenderly, for he
Knows what the pain of stifled things can be.

I know that this is true. God does treat these little
ones with special care and they grow up happily in
the spirit world. Away from the spite, the petty mean-
nesses and tensions of our earthly world, they mature
into truly beautiful men and women.

I was privileged to see my daughter, now grown up
in the spirit world, and I couldn't believe that this
lovely creature with the long, chestnut hair curling
round her shoulders, could actually belong to me. I
was so proud of her.

People find it easier to understand the grief of a
mother who has lost a baby born alive, but destined
to breathe only a little while. Yet even the understanding of family and friends doesn't seem to ease
the burden. Strangely enough, a poem can sometimes
help where all the well-meaning attentions of friends
do not.

Mrs T.C. of Middlesex told me her sad story when
she wrote to say how comforting she had found a
poem given to me by the spirit world and printed in
an earlier book.

Dear Doris,
First of all I would like to thank you for your

poem *In A Baby Castle*, which has helped me enormously in the last seven months. It has helped me accept my baby's death.

Seven months ago I had a baby boy called Daniel, who was born premature at twenty-six weeks. I prayed so hard that he would live, so did my family. The doctors and nurses did everything they could to save him but sadly there was nothing more they could do and after five days he passed away.

Those five days I sat there watching my son fight for his life were the worst. Just sitting there knowing he was going to die and not being able to do anything for him. I felt so useless.

On the fifth morning the nurse came to get me and said it was getting near his time and asked me if I would like to hold him for the last time on my own in a quiet room. I agreed because I knew he was going to die and I couldn't cope waiting any more. I went into the other room and five minutes later she brought Daniel to me. That is a memory I will treasure for ever. He was so beautiful.

I miss him very much and wish I could have him back. I've always wanted a child of my own and now the hospital isn't sure if I will be able to have another one but I'm going to try.

I am sending you a copy of the poem I wrote for Daniel a few weeks after he died. I hope you like it, I just wrote down how I felt one day and my mum suggested I sent it to you.

Yours sincerely,
Mrs T.C.

Darling Daniel

You're all we ever wanted, but it just wasn't to
　　be.
But we were together for a few days
Just you, Dad and me.

You made us so very happy
And proud that you chose us,
And we will never forget
The happiness you gave us.

When we held you in our arms
I can't explain the love
Never wanting to let go
Although we knew we must.

So beautiful and perfect
In every single way
But we'll be together again
All three of us some day.

Though our hearts are aching
And we long to hold you tight
We'll visit you in our dreams
When we go to sleep at night.

So many things we want to say,
To show how much we care,
And in our minds we really know
That you will always be there.

So please don't ever forget us,
'Cos we will never forget you,

We just hope that you are happy
In everything you do.

So 'bye now our darling
We'll see you again some day
When we can tell you all the things
We are really trying to say.

Love Mum and Dad

My eyes fill with tears whenever I read that poignant poem and I marvel once again at the courage and dignity of so called 'ordinary' people. I know just what those poor parents are going through and I'm glad that at least they have the comfort of knowing that their little Daniel is not lost and gone for ever.

Mrs D.M. of London sent me another moving poem on the same subject. She lost her little son after just twelve short hours and has suffered years of turmoil and heartache ever since. But at last she has come to terms with the tragedy.

Do you ever wonder why he was born so very
   small,
And do you ever ask yourself why he was given
to you at all,
Do you ever wonder what you did to deserve
the pain,
And was it ever really worth the strain,
Did you ever feel alone and think that no one
   cared,

And knew they really wanted to but never really
    dared.
Do you ever wonder why you still cry so many
    tears,
And never thought the hurt would last for all
    those many years.
Do you ever feel that your life keeps going
    wrong,
And wonder what it is in you that helps to keep
    you strong,
Do you ever ask just why it should have
    happened to you,
And will the memory of then, remain your
    whole life through,
And even if you could turn back time and had
    the chance to erase that day
You know that even with all the hurt – you'd
    have it no other way.

But it's not just bereaved parents who need our
love and understanding. We should also spare a
thought for the parents of handicapped children. I
particularly liked this poem from Mrs D.W. of Llanelli,
who wrote: 'All children are special, Doris, but the
handicapped child gives so much and asks for so little,
only love.'

The Gift Of A Special Child

A talk was held quite far from earth
'It's time again for another birth.'
Said the angels to the Lord above,

This special child will need much love,
His progress may seem very slow,
Accomplishments he may not show,
And he may need much extra care,
From all the folks he meets down there;
He may not learn nor laugh nor play,
His thoughts may seem quite far away,
In many ways he won't adapt
He will be known as handicapped.
So let's be careful where he's sent
We want his life to be content.
Please Lord find parents who
Will do this special job for you.
They will not gather right away
The leading note they're asked to play,
But with this child sent from above
Comes stronger faith and richer love
And soon they'll know the privilege given
In caring for this child from heaven
That special child so meek and mild
Is heaven's very special child.

I get a lot of poems about children but they don't make up my entire postbag by any means. Recently I've been very pleased to see a great feeling for old people reflected in the lines. Pleased, not because I'm getting on a bit myself these days(!), but because of the dreadful attacks on pensioners that we keep reading about. I really can't believe some of the things that happen now. Twenty years ago the most hardened villain wouldn't stoop to attacking a defenceless old lady. How things have changed.

Yet, judging from my post, I know that old people

are still loved and appreciated in many, many homes.
Mrs C.W. from Sussex sent me these charming verses:

My Gran

I wish my Gran were here with me
And not gone into Heaven,
She'd be quite flabbergasted
How I've grown now I am seven.

I 'member how she used to say
That I was just knee high
And how she wiped my tears away
When people made me cry.

My Grannie never made me cry
She kissed my tears away
And it was lovely when she said
'My dear, let's go and play.'

I 'member how she used to wear
A funny little hat
And she wasn't 'zactly thin
And yet she wasn't 'zactly fat.

But she was round and cuddly
Just like my teddy bear
And I'd climb upon her lap
When she sat in the big armchair.

She'd throw her arms around me,
Give me such a squashy squeeze.
If you're listening Jesus
Oh do send her back – oh please.

I'm sure that you don't need my Gran
As half as much as me
There must be lots of other grans
Up there for you to see.

And never any tears for Gran
To wipe away up there
'Cos no one cries in Heaven –
Well – perhaps they mustn't dare . . .

I'm glad to see that elderly aunties are also appreciated. Mrs E.O. of Devon was inspired to write this poem on the very evening that her much loved old auntie passed over. *Invisible Me* shows great understanding.

Invisible Me

You think that I am gone, because you cannot see
Or hear the footfall that was me!
I am only near,
I can see and I can hear.
I wish that you – when you think of me
Would speak to me and say my name and see
There is another life for you and me.
You cannot see the air or touch the breeze,
You cannot touch the wind but hear it in the
    trees.
You know it's there because you hear and feel
But in God's good time, he will reveal
All these wonders to you, dear.

So do not be afraid, be of good cheer,
Your loved ones are waiting for you here.
The Lord's my shepherd and He's yours,
He opens all these doors.
I have simply left you for a while
And you cannot see my smile
But when you need me I'll be there
To help you and show you that I care.

So think of me as I used to be
When I was young, well and free
From pain, infirmity and age
Which held my soul within a cage.

The Good Shepherd held the key
And only He
Could open wide the door
And set me free.

A little while I am with you,
And then I go to those I knew
So many years ago
Who shared my life and loved me so.
So do not grieve for me, my dear, as on your way
    you go.

My last poem has the rather sombre title of *Death*.
But don't be put off. Once again the work is unsigned,
but the words suggest to me that they were written
by someone who has been very close to death and has
good reason to know that it is nothing to fear.

191

Death

I lie here on a bed of leaves
Watching birds fly thro' the trees
Autumn will soon be here they say
With falling leaves which soon decay
But though these leaves are dying fast
Death itself – it does not last
All living things that grow and thrive
Will never die – all will survive
There is life in another world
Where joy and love are all unfurled.

Many of us fear to die
But this is truth – it is no lie
Do not fear death, it is not bleak
Just drift into a nice warm sleep
I tried it once, but doctors fought
To save my life was their one thought
Now that I am fit and well
On these thoughts I should not dwell
But all of you who fear to die
Believe me now, I tell no lie
I do not mean you to deceive
But in these things I do believe.

When I was very close to death
I could feel its comfort breath
It's warm and gentle, sweet and soft
Death itself holds no wrath
And so you see, when death is near
I'm sure that you will have no fear
Then you will only wish to die
And let your restless spirit fly

To learn of many things untold
As slowly wonders will unfold
I wish that this could comfort few
Who'd not fear death if they just knew.

So there we are. I hope you've enjoyed this selection of poems as much as I have.

Chapter Thirteen

'Now, Doris,' said the nurse, 'where on earth are we going to put these?'

She was carrying the most enormous basket of flowers, nearly three feet high and absolutely stuffed to bursting with pink and white blooms – a beautiful gift from Terry.

'This place is like a flower stall already.'

'How about there?' I suggested, pointing to the shelf that ran parallel to my bed. 'If we move the cards and shift that chair a bit ...'

The nurse bustled about and, a few deft moves later, the basket was safely installed in pride of place only inches from my feet and the cards were squashed together at the other end of the shelf.

Yes, as you've probably guessed by now, I'm finishing yet another book from my hospital bed and this time I seem to be worse than ever.

To tell the truth, I haven't been well for some time, but there have been so many bugs going around that I assumed I was falling for one thing after another. After all, I do seem to have this nasty habit of catching everything going.

I even began to wonder if I could be suffering from a form of agoraphobia because my symptoms became dramatically worse when I went out.

Not long ago I was thrilled to be invited to a royal film première. I was so looking forward to it. It's been years since I've seen a film at the cinema and this affair was to be much more exciting than an ordinary night at the pictures. The Royal Family and countless stars were to be present, all dressed up to the nines. It would be a truly glittering occasion.

I treated myself to a beautiful new dress made of real silk, I had my hair done specially, my nails painted and, although I don't wear much make-up, I spent ages fiddling with my powder and lipstick.

By the time I'd finished I looked pretty smart considering, and John, too, was elegant in evening dress. We certainly wouldn't be letting the side down when we mixed with all those posh people.

But it wasn't to be.

During the afternoon a fuzzy headache had come on and I wasn't feeling 100 per cent but I put it down to excitement.

'You'll be all right when you get there, Doris,' I told myself firmly. I was quite determined to go.

Well, admittedly, I did go. It was just that I didn't stay!

Hardly had I sat down in my plush cinema seat, than the room started spinning and I felt so ill I thought I would pass out.

'It's no good, John, I'm going to have to go home,' I whispered to John who was sitting beside me. I would have sobbed with disappointment had I not been feeling so dreadful.

So John helped me to my feet and I struggled back up the aisle and out to the foyer where the stars were still arriving. I was just in time to see Joan Collins waft past in something extremely glamorous and then I

195

was back in the car, heading for home.

Instead of hob-nobbing with celebrities in my silk dress, I spent the evening with my feet up, drinking tea in my dressing-gown. I never did get to see a single frame of the film.

Yet the next day my faithful doctor couldn't find anything obviously wrong with me.

'It must be all in the mind, Doris,' I told myself. But it was hard to believe. The symptoms were so real and physical. 'Yes, but that's what happens,' the nurse in me replied, 'the symptoms are real enough but your mind brings them on. I wonder if it could be agoraphobia?'

Now I believe that this is exactly what can happen in some cases of agoraphobia but in my case it wasn't agoraphobia. Over the next few weeks my health seesawed wildly. One minute I wasn't feeling too bad at all, the next I could hardly move. After a while, though, I couldn't help noticing that the trend was downwards. Sittings and public engagements had to be postponed and the doctor gave me antibiotics because, on top of everything else, I seemed to be suffering with a sinus infection.

Then at Easter I collapsed again. It had reached the stage where I was so dizzy I could hardly stand up. I thought the infection must have spread to my inner ear, which affects balance, but the doctor was not happy.

'You can't go on like this, Doris,' he said. 'You'll have to go back to hospital, and this time you must stay there until they've sorted you out.'

By now I felt so awful I was willing to agree. So back I went to hospital, and after a couple of days of tests they finally discovered what was wrong with me.

I had a brain tumour.

At once everything fell into place. The out-of-character fainting at Christmas, the dizziness, the headaches and all the peculiar illnesses that had plagued me ever since. They all stemmed from the same cause.

I had a brain tumour. They are frightening words, brain tumour, but these days surgeons are so clever and it seems I am lucky. My tumour is operable. So here I am sitting in my hospital bed waiting for the operation.

Fortunately, I had just about finished this book when I was admitted so that's a load off my mind. I'd hate to be late for the publishers' deadline.

What's more, the rest has done me good. The nurses are very kind and under their gentle care I've been feeling better.

Flowers and cards have poured in and I don't have time to be lonely. I've had loads of visitors. Derek Jameson and his wife, Ellen, called in a little while ago with a lovely teddy bear to cheer me up because they knew I'd have so many flowers. Freddie Starr has promised to fly over in his helicopter and when I'm short of official visitors the nurses pop in for a chat.

One American girl was so excited when she heard about my work that, even though she wasn't on duty, she came to see me. She was fascinated to hear more about the spirit world because apparently on a recent visit to a supposedly haunted house in London, she photographed her sister standing next to an ancient fireplace. When the film was developed they could clearly see another figure standing beside her, even though there was no one visible at the time.

'Yes, that's quite possible, love,' I told her, and I

went on to explain about the christening photograph in which a likeness of John Michael as a baby showed clearly in the air between me and the child who was named that day.

All in all, it's not too bad here in hospital. I can't pretend I'm not nervous about the operation. I expect I shall be out of action for quite a while afterwards and they will have to shave my head, which is upsetting for any woman, even one of my age.

Still, I won't be beaten. I've ordered a set of the prettiest turbans and the next time you see me I expect I'll have an exotic eastern look.

Wish me luck!

Doris passed away peacefully on May 8th 1987, nearly two weeks after a six-and-a-half-hour operation to remove a brain tumour. She never regained consciousness.

Two days before the operation she was still working on this book, organizing her family and bravely trying to keep up her own spirits and those of the people around her.

The operation was scheduled for that Saturday.

'Oh well, on Sunday I shall either be here or I won't,' she said cheerfully.

In fact this was one of the few occasions when Doris was wrong. On Sunday she was here, and yet she wasn't. She survived the operation only to slip gently away thirteen days later.

Despite her brave words, Doris was frightened at the thought of this operation. She wasn't afraid of dying. As she always said: 'There is no death. You can't die for the life of you.' No, what worried her was her possible condition after the operation. She had been warned that her memory might be impaired for a while and that, temporarily, she might be unable to speak.

Doris was no fool and she was also a trained nurse. Reading between the lines she feared that she might be left blind, dumb or 'stupid'.

Had any of those things happened she would have faced them with the courage and humour with which she faced every problem that came her way. But inside she would have been crying.

How much better this way. After all the illnesses and operations she had endured, she finally slipped away without further pain or suffering. Now we can only hope that she's happy at last; walking with her father and John Michael, the beloved son she missed so much, in the bright fields of the spirit world.

200

Epilogue

Throughout her life, Doris brought comfort and hope to thousands of bereaved people. She also gave generously of her time and money to those in need. But perhaps the best possible tribute to Doris is to let her work speak for itself.

Here, with the kind permission of Mrs Carol Harrison, is a transcript of Doris' last sitting. Mrs Harrison lost her son, Stuart, in the Zeebrugge ferry disaster. When the sitting took place on April 8th 1987 Doris was already very ill but she was determined not to let the family down. Her only worry was that her health might spoil the sitting. This is what happened:

DORIS: They're singing Happy Birthday so there's a birthday coming or a birthday just been.

CAROL: It was my birthday a couple of weeks ago, on March 13th.

DORIS: He's singing Happy Birthday. He's only young. Possibly about nineteen. It's a very young voice.

CAROL: He was seventeen.

DORIS: Something about he shouldn't have been there. Does that make sense to you?

CAROL: That's right. He didn't have permission from his college to go.

DORIS: Who's Betty? He wants to send his love to Betty.

CAROL: Betty is his grandmother.

DORIS: Who's David? It's a 'd' sound, 'd', 'd', 'd' ...

CAROL: Dean. That's my son's best friend.

DORIS: He's talking about someone called Anne. You've been talking to her about him.

CAROL: Yes, Anne's my friend.

DORIS: The awful part is that I needn't have been there, he's saying. I nearly didn't go. He went to please someone. So whether he wanted to keep someone company, I don't know. There were five of them.

CAROL: He went to please some friends but there were four of them not five.

DORIS: Oh there were meant to be five but one didn't go.

CAROL: That's right.

DORIS: We're all right. That's what he wants to get over. It all happened very quickly. Now that was something to do with an anniversary coming. It's someone's anniversary. Who's Paul? I've met Paul.

CAROL: Paul is my friend's son. He died when he was six and a half. His anniversary is coming up on April 19th.

DORIS: Doesn't he get excited? He's talking very fast and his old hands go. Who's Tony or Tommy? Tommy's been talking about me, he says.

CAROL: Tommy's a friend.

DORIS: He's met Bill or Bert over there ... it's a 'b'

sound. That wasn't Bernard, love, was it?'

CAROL: Bernard was the pet name of the friend who died with him.

DORIS: He's talking about someone called Alison. She was talking about him. And Mark or Martin.

CAROL: Alison is my niece and Mark and Martin are his stepbrothers.

DORIS: (*To Karen, Stuart's sister*) Are you going to get married soon?

KAREN: No.

DORIS: I'm sure he said you were getting engaged.

[CAROL: Karen has since got engaged.]*

DORIS: Who's Annette? A … A …

KAREN: I know an Angela.

DORIS: No. No, it's not Annette, it's Andy.

CAROL: His stepfather.

DORIS: Why didn't you say your dad? Oh, you didn't call him Dad, always Andy.

CAROL: That's right.

DORIS: He's a lovely-looking boy with such a cheeky grin and a dimple here. He says, I was a bit of a bugger sometimes but I did love you all. The point is, you don't know till you come this side. They never say I love you. They think it's sissy. It's only when they get here. I know, lovey, and they do understand. Who's Rose or Ron …?

CAROL: My aunt and my grandmother were both called Rose.

DORIS: He's telling me something about a watch. Was he wearing a new watch? He's a bit annoyed

---

*Square brackets indicate comments added by Mrs Harrison since the sitting.

203

about that. I'd just bought a new watch, he said.

CAROL: He did need one.

DORIS: I don't suppose it'll be any good now, love. Who's Claire? Susanne ... Try that again ... Susan ... all I can hear you going is ssss. She's on the spirit side.

CAROL: Our friends' daughter was called Samantha. She died the Sunday before Stuart. He went to her funeral the day before he died.

DORIS: You tell Sam's mum that she's all right. Julie ... There's going to be a baby born and he's laughing his head off about this. She doesn't think he knows.

[CAROL: Julie is his cousin. She's now pregnant.]

DORIS: He's a very caring young boy. He said, will you please tell my mum and family ... You're a bit embarrassed, love. Go on ... Don't let them spend a lot of money. I'm not there. You know I'm alive and our love's alive. Don't spend a lot of money ... He bites his nails, doesn't he? And you're dark but he's sort of sandy. I can see him.

KAREN: Ginger.

DORIS: Well, I wasn't going to say that because I thought he might be offended. Strawberry blond, he said. Who's Phillip? Try again, I haven't got it right ... Frank ... no, you've missed it, darling. Don't worry about it. It's a bit confusing because he keeps dashing off to have a look what's going on. I was so angry at first when I got over, he says. He'd some nice friends at last because deep down he was very shy. Gary – who's Gary?

CAROL: Gary was his other best friend.

DORIS: Tell him I've been back, though he'll never believe it! Oh. I don't think I ought to say

204

that, darling. Well all right. He says, the old fella, (he thinks the world of you), he needs a new car, you know. Well when you get that money, you buy yourself a new car for me. If I have had to give up my life, then for God's sake let me help the people I love. So will you promise me that, Dad? He's never had a new car in his life and I'm going to buy him one.

[CAROL: My husband did need a new car, but Doris wasn't to know that as we turned up at her house in my daughter's boyfriend's new turbo.]

DORIS: That was a name beginning with P ... a girl's name ... Penelope ... no, Pauline.

CAROL: Pauline is Samantha's mum.

DORIS: Then there was a 'b' sound. Who worked in a shop? He's here too, so don't think the boy's on his own.

CAROL: My uncle had a butcher's shop. He died a few weeks before Stuart.

DORIS: I don't know, sweetheart. Did you? Now I don't want to harass you but I think they would like me to ask you this one question, then we'll leave it alone because it's going to be bad enough over the next few days. Was it very long? Mum, I've got to be truthful, he says. I was very frightened and I got separated. I think I was holding onto Nicola for a while, then we were separated. I remember we laughed at first. We thought it was funny when the ship started tipping. Then it happened so quickly, but I know you have been asking. It happened very quickly. The cold and no air and I quickly went to sleep. We had been down to the car and I went off and that's when we got separated.

[CAROL: Our neighbours who took Stuart were in the morgue when we went to Zeebrugge, but Stuart wasn't found until five weeks later.]

DORIS: Who's Amy or Ada? It's a short name, only three letters.

CAROL: Ivy, Stuart's grandmother.

DORIS: Oh, that's it. He's got an accent, lovey. I'm not being rude.

[CAROL: Stuart had a Somerset accent.]

DORIS: I can't very well say that, either. They get angry with me but they forget I'm a stranger to you. Can I be personal, love? (*To Karen*) Have you taken a ring off? Were you engaged before?

KAREN: I was nearly engaged before.

DORIS: That's it because he wasn't very happy about that. He's glad you finished with the boy. Who's Ed?

CAROL: Ed is Samantha's dad.

DORIS: Will you tell Ed that we've been back. He's going on about that new car again. He's determined you're going to have it. He loves you. He said, I wasn't demonstrative, Doris, I would just say, 'Cheerio,' and half the time I didn't even say that, I just used to go. I regret that now. I didn't go up and give Mum a hug. It's a pity you have to come over here before you can say the things you want to say. Listen, he says, and he's pointing at me. Never be afraid to tell people you love them because when anything like this happens and you come over this side it's too bloody late. My dad's so easy-going he never used to chase us up. Why didn't I tell him how much I appreciated him? He was always there. He never pushed me. I had a marvellous family.

Well I still have. Yes, you still have, love, but you get it off your chest, that's what we're trying for. Don't keep wandering, sweetheart. I hope I've got that right, lovey. Forgive me if I haven't but it's a bit difficult with this pain in my ears. Sometimes I don't hear so well. They all came from the same place so they're all going to be together. It will be rather splendid, he said. Yes it will, love. We have heard them discussing it and everyone's in agreement that we all be put to rest together. Is that right, love?

[CAROL: They were all going to be buried together. Both families wanted it. We had already chosen their plots before seeing Doris.]

DORIS: Tell them all that's only our old overcoats and we'll all be there to make sure you do everything right. He's laughing. He's got a real old belly laugh and he makes it light. Tell them I've met Arthur.

[CAROL: This name meant nothing but my husband was adopted and did not know his family.]

DORIS: They don't know Arthur, love. Something to do with a solicitor … I think you've got yourself in a bit of a muddle, love. Or it might be me. Now that was something to do with cooking. Do you cook for a living?

CAROL: Stuart did. He was training to be a chef.

DORIS: Oh that's it. He keeps saying cooking, you know, for a living. He didn't say it was him. Oh, he says he was going to be a steward.

CAROL: He wanted to be a steward on a liner. He told us that a few weeks before he died.

DORIS: He was looking forward to this. Then that was Alec or Alan.

CAROL: Allen is Dean's surname – his best friend.

DORIS: (*To Carol and Andy who are getting emotional*) I know, love. Don't think I don't feel for you. I have lost four children myself so I know what it's like, love. I don't care what anybody says. You can lose a father, a mother, but until you have lost a child no one can tell you. Nobody knows. D'you know, John Michael would be forty-three on August 7th and there's never a day goes past without me thinking of him. Even with all I know, there's always an empty place there. But the sun does shine again. Honestly. I promise you. Now he's saying, stop being morbid, you. There's no need to be morbid. They've got enough on their plates without you being morbid. What were you going to tell me, love, then I will listen to you? You always wanted to travel so it's not been wasted. I can go anywhere in the world, look at anything I want to look at. Who's James? J … J … Joseph … John. It's John living. I can just hear the J.

CAROL: His stepfather's real name is John.

DORIS: I know you are very quiet, love, but there's such a bond between you. You shouldn't tell me that, love. He says, I wasn't meant to happen. The point is, love, you had a good life. I was a bit difficult at times, he says, I was no angel. It took me a little while before I settled down. Then this had to happen. It's not fair, is it? No, I don't think it is either, love. Who's Bill?

CAROL: A family friend.

DORIS: And Kathy?

CAROL: My friend.

DORIS: Who's Barry?

CAROL: His uncle.

DORIS: I think that was Stephen. I was not sure about that ... S ... It couldn't be Stuart, could it? [CAROL: At this point, Doris didn't know Stuart's name.]

DORIS: That's what I've been waiting for. I'm all right, Dad. I'm not dead, honest. I know it's a great wrench because, let's face it, I was a bit of a trial sometimes, but you never ever grumbled. Thank you for being such a wonderful family. Now don't cry, love, or you'll upset me. Not bloody fair, he keeps saying. He uses bloody quite a bit, doesn't he, love? They told me before you came to be brave for the sake of my parents but it's not bloody fair. I know, love, but you will be able to help the others a lot. You've got me crying now and usually I can manage to control it. Sorry about that, he said. But I know what you're going through ... Believe me, the sun does shine again ... I don't know how long it'll take ... I've been there. I know what it's like to get up in the morning and think, 'Oh God, I've got to face another day.' What you've got to remember, love, is you've got to take it day by day, one step at a time. And one day you'll wake up and, this I promise you, the sun will be shining again in your heart. You'll know with absolute certainty that your Stuart and all his friends, they are alive. But at the moment it's a cross that nobody else can carry for you. It's bad enough to lose a child without having all this agony piled on the top. At least I was able to hold my baby in my arms until my father collected him. I think they've already found him, but you've got to

209

prepare yourselves for the fact that you probably won't be able to see him.

[CAROL: They had found Stuart the very day we went to see Doris. His face had been slammed against something and that is why they told us not to see him.]

DORIS: Don't remember him as you think he might look now. Hold a picture in your mind of the way he went out to work every day and think about how he was on the earth, because that's how he is now, lovey. You've already hung two new photographs up.

[CAROL: Yes, we had put up two new photos.]

DORIS: Oh yes, I know what you're up to, he says. One of them's not too bad but the other one I'm not so sure about, but me mum likes it. Don't you worry, I'm keeping an eye on you. He says, say hello to Paddy. Hello Paddy, love. He says, I'm not vindictive but you make sure they pay. They've got to be made to pay because that was sheer bloody negligence. When you went up to Stuart's room he said he'd been trying on sweaters and he's left two on the bed.

CAROL: Yes. Karen put away two sweaters that were on his bed.

DORIS: Sh ... sh ... Sheila. No, try again ... Sharon.

CAROL: Sharon was a girl at college.

DORIS: Well I think you'll find you'll be hearing from her. It was so dark and so cold, he says. That was the worst part of it, trying to find each other in the dark. He held a child. She was only a toddler.

CAROL: Stuart would have helped a child. He loved them and they loved him.

DORIS: And then we got swept apart. That was the last thing I remember. I must keep this baby up ... Oh what a dreadful shame ... Well never mind, love ... But there was one child left behind in Nicola's family.

CAROL: The son Patrick, aged twenty, was left.

DORIS: So his whole family's been wiped out. It breaks my heart. But I know that they're alive. You've only got to put your hand out and they'll hold on. I know it's the physical presence we grieve for. I'm just the same. When my babies died, and if my husband was to go before me I'd still be the same, as much as I know that we'll all be together again. But still you have to carry that cross. Don't bottle it up, love, because tears are God's healing gift to us. Bottle it up inside you and you'll go mad. It's not much consolation, I know, but at least you know there's so many people in the same boat as you. You're not alone and you know that each family is thinking of you as you're thinking of them. Now why does he keep going on about the dog? It's the dog's birthday.

[CAROL: Karen had been singing Happy Birthday to the dog before we went to see Doris.]

DORIS: Give her a cuddle for me, he says, because he loves that dog. He idolizes Karen. I just said, isn't she a beautiful girl, and he said, I think so. I know, we all say things and do things and it's only when something like this happens we think, I shouldn't have shouted, I shouldn't have said that. But that's human nature, lovey, and they understand. When we go over there the love link gets stronger and stronger. Dad, promise me you'll get a new car. Get a good one and when you go out I'll be sitting there with you. Are you a hairdresser, Karen?

KAREN: Yes.

DORIS: 'Cos I said, what does she do, your sister, and he said, she works in a salon. She's a hairdresser.

Well, I'll have to let you go, because if the doctor comes in and finds me working he'll do his pieces. But I couldn't let you down again. (*A previously arranged visit had had to be cancelled owing to Doris' poor health*)

I'm sorry it's been a bit bitty but working through this pain has been difficult.

Carol Harrison sent Doris this tape with her love and thanks, for the hope and peace of mind she'd given the family. She also enclosed a poem which she thought Doris would enjoy. Strangely enough, unknown to Carol at the time she sat down to write her letter, Doris had already passed away. Yet the poem echoes Doris' beliefs perfectly. This is what Doris would have wanted to say had she been in a position to speak for herself. She couldn't have wished for a better ending to her last book.

Don't Weep For Me Here

If I should reach heaven before you,
Remember, don't weep for me here
For I shall be happy with Jesus
With never a worry or fear.

We journey along on life's highway,
The future unknown to us all,
We know not the day or the hour
The time when the saviour may call.

Together we've laboured for Jesus,
What happiness year after year!
So if I'm promoted to glory,
Remember don't weep for me here.

I'll watch for you coming to glory,
To be with my saviour so dear,
If I should reach heaven before you,
Remember, don't weep for me here.

All Futura Books are available at your bookshop or newsagent, or can be ordered from the following address: Futura Books, Cash Sales Department, P.O. Box 11, Falmouth, Cornwall TR10 9EN.

Please send cheque or postal order (no currency), and allow 60p for postage and packing for the first book plus 25p for the second book and 15p for each additional book ordered up to a maximum charge of £1.90 in U.K.

B.F.P.O. customers please allow 60p for the first book, 25p for the second book plus 15p per copy for the next 7 books, thereafter 9p per book

Overseas customers, including Eire, please allow £1.25 for postage and packing for the first book, 75p for the second book and 28p for each subsequent title ordered.